T0268319

"This not just another book on Calvin but a p
of the life and doctrine of the Genevan refori
is made clear, classic misunderstandings are cleared up and put aside, and the
picture of a man devoted to serving God and the church is painted as a mirror
to the reader."

Herman Selderhuis, professor of church history at the Theological University of
Apeldoorn and president of the Reformation Research Consortium

"Anyone interested in exploring the life and thought of John Calvin will welcome
this book! Thianto is a veteran scholar and teacher of Calvin who guides us
step by step to understand Calvin's life and context as well as the dynamic
theology that motivated readers of his magnum opus, the *Institutes of the
Christian Religion.* Thianto presents each of the four 'books' of the *Institutes,*
providing clear discussions of their major theological insights. Primarily,
the *Institutes* provide a way of understanding God's revelation in Holy
Scripture. As such, Calvin's thought has had a lasting impact on the global
church. His views also nurture Christian living. Thianto's book helps us understand Calvin's theology and ways his insights can be significant for us today!"

Donald K. McKim, author of *John Calvin: A Companion to His Life and Theology*
and *Coffee with Calvin: Daily Devotions*

"*An Explorer's Guide to John Calvin* is an appealing introduction to one of the
Reformation's most influential figures. Countering many modern misconcep-
tions about the Genevan reformer, Yudha Thianto presents Calvin as a man of
his times and also as a profound theologian who still speaks to Christians today.
Thianto's lively and sympathetic portrait of Calvin's life and theology is an ideal
starting point for those wanting to learn more about the origins of Calvinism."

Amy Nelson Burnett, Varner Professor of History at the University of
Nebraska-Lincoln

"In a culmination of years of teaching and scholarship, with genuine warmth
and affection, Yudha Thianto introduces us to John Calvin, his friend. Even for
those familiar with Calvin, this is a fresh, faithful, and accessible guide. Thianto
effortlessly dispels myths, depolarizes caricatures, and deepens Calvin the
person, pastor, and Reformer. For the uninitiated, this book is an outstanding
introduction to Calvin and his best-known work, *Institutes of the Christian
Religion* (1559), and includes a whole chapter dedicated to frequently asked
questions that range from theological concepts to Calvin and his controversies.
You will not be disappointed."

Jessica Joustra, assistant professor of religion and theology at Redeemer University

"Introductions to Calvin are a dime a dozen. What distinguishes this volume is its attention to historical context, its detailed coverage of major themes found in the *Institutes*, and its readability. It is a fine work by a fine scholar and will reward careful and reflective reading!"

Jon Balserak, senior lecturer in early modern religion at the University of Bristol

"In this engaging book, Reformation scholar Yudha Thianto provides a perceptive and sympathetic introduction to the life and theology of the Genevan reformer John Calvin. Here readers will discover important clues explaining Calvin's formidable influence in the sixteenth century—and why his legacy continues to be important in our own day."

Scott M. Manetsch, professor of church history at Trinity Evangelical Divinity School and associate general editor of the Reformation Commentary on Scripture

"Yudha Thianto provides us with a warm introduction to his friend across the centuries, John Calvin. He contextualizes him, unfolds his life story, and then walks us carefully through his *Institutes*. You'll find this slim volume packed with the essential facts to know about Calvin and his famed magnum opus. A delightfully readable introduction to the sixteenth-century French refugee, pastor, and theologian."

Gwenfair Walters Adams, professor of church history and chair of the Division of Christian Thought at Gordon-Conwell Theological Seminary

"In 1539, John Calvin penned a short note to readers of his *Institutes of the Christian Religion*, explaining his circumstances for preparing another version of the work that more than any other defined him in the world's eyes, and commenting on what he believed was its value. Calvin recognized the necessity of having a guide for approaching the Scriptures—that an unprepared reader might easily stumble. Now, Yudha Thianto has provided a similar guide to Calvin's *Institutes*. Written in a familiar style, as if explaining the thought of a close friend, Thianto confidently leads his readers through meeting John Calvin as an early modern thinker and a pastor, then illuminates the path through the *Institutes* itself."

R. Ward Holder, professor of theology and director of the honors program at Saint Anselm College

"Calvin's theology is best understood in the context of his life, and this helpful guide introduces us to both. Calvin comes across as a faithful pastor and careful expositor of Holy Scripture, a teacher of the church who we can honor in no better way than to listen to him. Highly recommended!"

Timothy George, distinguished professor at Beeson Divinity School of Samford University and general editor of the Reformation Commentary on Scripture

An Explorer's Guide to

JOHN CALVIN

YUDHA THIANTO

Academic

An imprint of InterVarsity Press
Downers Grove, Illinois

InterVarsity Press
P.O. Box 1400 | Downers Grove, IL 60515-1426
ivpress.com | email@ivpress.com

©2022 by Yudha Thianto

All rights reserved. No part of this book may be reproduced in any form without written permission
from InterVarsity Press.

InterVarsity Press® is the publishing division of InterVarsity Christian Fellowship/USA®.
For more information, visit intervarsity.org.

Scripture quotations, unless otherwise noted, are from the New Revised Standard Version Bible,
copyright © 1989 National Council of the Churches of Christ in the United States of America.
Used by permission. All rights reserved worldwide.

The publisher cannot verify the accuracy or functionality of website URLs used in this book
beyond the date of publication.

Cover design and image composite: David Fassett
Interior design: Beth McGill

ISBN 978-1-5140-0126-4 (print) | ISBN 978-1-5140-0127-1 (digital)

Printed in the United States of America ∞

Library of Congress Cataloging-in-Publication Data
Names: Thianto, Yudha, 1965- author.
Title: An explorer's guide to John Calvin / Yudha Thianto.
Description: Downers Grove, IL : IVP Academic, [2022] | Series: Explorer's
   guide | Includes bibliographical references and index.
Identifiers: LCCN 2022007909 (print) | LCCN 2022007910 (ebook) | ISBN
   9781514001264 (paperback) | ISBN 9781514001271 (ebook)
Subjects: LCSH: Calvin, Jean, 1509-1564. | Calvin, Jean, 1509-1564.
   Institutio Christianae religionis.
Classification: LCC BX9418 .T45 2022 (print) | LCC BX9418 (ebook) | DDC
   284/.2092–dc23/eng/20220321
LC record available at https://lccn.loc.gov/2022007909
LC ebook record available at https://lccn.loc.gov/2022007910

26   25   24   23   22 | 6   5   4   3   2   1

To the memory of

my father and mother,

who first taught me to live out

the Reformed faith without being dogmatic.

Contents

Acknowledgments

This book started with a conversation with David McNutt, Academic Editor of IVP Academic, at a conference in October 2018. There he asked me if I would be interested in writing a book to introduce readers with very little or no prior knowledge of John Calvin to this sixteenth-century Reformer. At that time, having taught a course on Calvin and the *Institutes* at Trinity Christian College fifteen times, I accepted the invitation without hesitation. It has been a joy to work closely with David in the publication of this book, and for this I am very thankful to him.

The entire Trinity Christian College community has been supportive of me in this writing project from start to finish. The college awarded me with a summer research grant to write a portion of this book. Considering the college-level readership for which the book is primarily intended, Provost Aaron Kuecker provided me with as much space as I needed to incorporate the project into my work with students both inside and outside the classroom. My colleagues in the theology department, Ben Ribbens and Keith Starkenburg, consistently encouraged me in the journey of the writing process, especially during the difficult months as we faced the coronavirus pandemic. Several friends and colleagues at Trinity Christian College and Hope Christian Reformed Church deserve special mention for their help and valuable encouragement as I wrote this book: Aron Reppmann, Mark Peters, Bob Rice, Diana Pell, Michael VanderWeele, Erick Sierra, Craig Mattson, Bill Boerman-Cornell, Dave Klanderman, Bill VanGroningen, and Roger Nelson. Students in my honors theology classes in the fall semesters of 2019 and 2020 read, discussed, and suggested improvements for some chapters of this book. As her Honors Work in the Major project, Avery Johnson read through the early completed draft of this book and gave me insightful notes on how to shape it to reach my intended readers well.

Finally, I would like to express my most sincere thanks to the H. Henry Meeter Center at Calvin University and Calvin Theological Seminary, and its director, Karin Maag, and curator, Paul Fields, without whose presence and assistance I would not have been able to write this book. The center has been a wonderful place for me to interact deeply with Calvin, Calvinism, and scholars' works from all over the world ever since I worked there as a student assistant during my years in the doctoral program at Calvin Theological Seminary. This interaction continues to be a strong foundation as I teach my classes and in writing the book you now hold. I sincerely hope that this book opens up more conversations on Calvin and his theology in the years to come.

Part One

Calvin
THE MAN

Why John Calvin?

A Tour Guide to Calvin

In this book, you will learn about my good friend John Calvin. I want you to get to know him because he has been a dear friend to me for so many years. Even though he lived about five centuries ago, I still hear his voice today. He is a person I go to when I need guidance in understanding the Bible, thinking about certain Christian teachings, getting ready to lead a worship service, teaching a Sunday school class, or thinking about life in general. I have listened to (or read, to be precise) many of his sermons, sung many psalms in the tunes that were first composed during his lifetime in Geneva, and prayed the prayers that he wrote. He has been my guide because he left behind a wealth of written work that is still valuable for us to learn from. Because he is a good friend of mine, I wanted to write a book about him so it can be a guide for you as you take a step into learning about him and his impact on Christianity since the time of the Reformation in the sixteenth century.

When you look at the number of books that Calvin wrote, including a shelf full of commentaries on the Bible, you may think it a daunting task to get to know him and his thoughts. Thankfully, we can gain insight into John Calvin by focusing on the final edition of his most famous work, *Institutes of the Christian Religion*, which he

Figure 1.1. A portrait of John Calvin

published in 1559. This work is massive. Even though it is one single publication, it is divided into four books with a total of eighty chapters. "How would I even start?" you might ask. I write this book as a response to your question. Imagine that I am serving you as your guide as you try to chart the landscape of Calvin's life and theology. You may compare the journey of understanding Calvin and his significance in the church as a trip to a vacation destination you have never visited before. In such a case, you need a tour guide.

The island of Bali, one of Indonesia's more than seventeen thousand islands, is famous for its beauty. It is one of the most-visited tourist destinations in the country. As a tropical island it offers scenery that can be breathtaking. The beaches are warm and inviting. If you love surfing, you will find places where you almost hear the waves call your name. If you love to see mountains and rice paddies rolling down their slopes, your eyes will delight in the greens of these fields. On the island there are volcanoes, some of which are still active, running right down its center. To the north, south, east, and west, you will find beaches and places to dive, do some snorkeling, or enjoy a boat ride. The music and dance performances will bring you to a whole different world when you visit the island.

But if it is your first time in Bali, you may find it hard to navigate. First, as is the traffic rule for the whole country of Indonesia, people drive on the left side of the street. You may be terrified when you drive on the island for the first time; all the other vehicles are coming toward you! Next, you may find it hard to pick where to start. Do you want to visit Kuta, the most famous beach on the island, first, and then go to Ubud, the mountain resort well known for its beauty, or should you reverse the order? Do you want to visit Besakih, the largest Hindu temple on the island, which has been around since the tenth century AD, on your first day or the last day? You have these questions, and to maximize your visit to the island, you need some guidance. After all, the island is quite large, about 2,300 square miles. A tour guide can help you navigate the area well so that you get the most out of your time there. In the same spirit, let me now be your guide to exploring the life and teaching of Calvin. This book will assist you to know Calvin as a person, a pastor, and a Reformer. It will also guide you to understand his main theological teachings as he explained them in the 1559 edition of his *Institutes of the Christian Religion.*

I grew up in Indonesia in a church that follows the teaching and practices that Calvin set forth when he was in Geneva in the sixteenth century. I still pause every now and then to ponder how wonderful it is that churches in modern-day Indonesia inherit so much from Calvin, a leader who lived several centuries ago in a land thousands of miles away. This is just a small example of how vast God's kingdom is. As a young boy, I was already familiar with Reformed theology, the teaching of the church that finds its roots in Calvin's teachings. I first encountered his *Institutes of the Christian Religion* when I was in high school. I still remember how the clarity and coherence of his thoughts mesmerized me. But it was not until I studied theology at Calvin Theological Seminary that I engaged myself in a deeper study of Calvin's life and theological thought. When I was doing my doctoral work, I studied under the guidance of Professor Richard Muller, who is well known for his academic works on Calvin, the Reformation, and the thoughts of numerous authors in the sixteenth and seventeenth centuries.

When I was a graduate student at Calvin Seminary, I had the opportunity to work as a student assistant at the H. Henry Meeter Center for Calvin Studies. The center is the largest in the world of its kind. It holds a collection of books and other material on John Calvin, Calvinism, the Reformation, and early modern studies. The center is jointly supported by Calvin Theological Seminary and Calvin University. As I worked at the center, I learned deeply about Calvin and his work. I also had numerous interactions with scholars, ministers, teachers, and students from all over the world. They came to the center to study and do research, and I still cherish my relationships with many of these people today.

FUN FACT

The H. Henry Meeter Center of Calvin University and Calvin Theological Seminary in Grand Rapids, Michigan, is a wonderful center for the study of Calvin and Calvinism. It holds about four hundred rare books published in the sixteenth century, including various editions of Calvin's *Institutes*, many of Calvin's other writings, books by other authors, and Bibles in various languages; about twenty-two thousand articles on Calvin, Calvinism, and the Reformation; several thousand microfilms and microfiches of early modern books and other material; and about 5,500 books on the same subjects.

When I completed this book, I was in my twentieth year of teaching theology at Trinity Christian College. In seventeen of those twenty years, I regularly taught a course on Calvin and his theology. At the beginning of each semester when I teach this course, I always ask my students—mostly juniors and seniors in college—whether there is a doctrine or a term that they (or other people they know) most associate with Calvin. The first doctrine that my students often mention is the doctrine of predestination. I'm not surprised; most Christians I know respond similarly. To many people, the name Calvin is almost synonymous with the doctrine of predestination. Many people think that he was the originator of this doctrine. Others believe that he invented the acronym TULIP. As we'll see, both of these ideas are mistaken.

What, then, are Calvin's most significant contributions as a theologian, and why should we continue to read his work today? Two reasons stand out to me: first, Calvin is a champion of biblical theology. And second, Calvin has made a lasting impact on the global church through his theological thought and his leadership.

Calvin as a Biblical Theologian

The term "biblical theology" means different things to different people. When I apply this term to my explanation of Calvin's significance, I mean that he is a thinker who builds all his theological thoughts firmly on the Bible. All of Calvin's doctrinal teachings start from his deep reading and study of the Bible. Beyond *Institutes of the Christian Religion* and other theological writings, Calvin left us with volumes upon volumes of Bible commentaries. In these commentaries he meticulously goes through each book verse by verse, explaining the meaning of each verse and passage carefully. Often the way he reads and interprets the Bible surprises me.

Calvin firmly believes that the Bible is the Word of God. He states that God has revealed himself first through his great work of creation and more specifically through his words in Scripture. He often uses the metaphor of spectacles to show that Scripture helps us to know God, just as a pair of spectacles helps a person with a vision problem to see or read better.[1] God gives us Scripture, Calvin believes, to show us the way into salvation and to give us the

---

[1] John Calvin, *Institutes of the Christian Religion* [1559], ed. John T. McNeill, trans. Ford Lewis Battles (Philadelphia: The Westminster Press, 1960), I.6.1.

privilege to know him intimately. Calvin states that Scripture holds
the highest authority over our lives because the Holy Spirit has
inspired the human authors to write God's words. Therefore, the
authority of Scripture comes directly from God. The Holy Spirit
also works in the hearts of people so that they can believe the Word
of God, and the Holy Spirit inwardly seals God's Word in their
hearts as it takes full charge of the whole person.[2] Here is where we
see Calvin's emphasis on the internal or inward testimony of the
Holy Spirit regarding Scripture.

Calvin insists that when we read and understand the Bible, we
must seek the plain sense or plain reading of Scripture. As much as
possible, he wants people to understand the words of Scripture as
they are written. He emphasizes this to avoid excessive allegorizing
of Scripture's meaning, which many medieval authors tended to do.
For this reason, Calvin worked very hard to write Bible commentaries based on his readings of the original languages of the Bible,
namely Hebrew and Greek. He did this because, in his time and
before, the church had a different way of interpreting the Bible.

Medieval exegesis and Calvin's approach. Beginning from the
medieval era, the church employed a four-layer method of interpreting Scripture. This method or approach is often called four-fold
exegesis. The medieval scholars believed that Scripture must be
interpreted following its literal, allegorical, tropological, and anagogical senses or meanings. The literal sense (or meaning) follows
the exact meaning of the words as written in the Bible. The allegorical sense refers to the meaning that is hidden beneath the
written words, namely a spiritual meaning not clearly seen in the
text. The tropological sense brings people to understand the moral
message of the written words. Last, the anagogical sense has to do
with what is still coming in the future, namely a look into the end

---

[2]Calvin, *Institutes* I.7.5.

of time and the second coming of Jesus. In theology we call the teaching of the second coming of Christ *eschatology.* Thus, the anagogical interpretation of Scripture carries with it the eschatological beliefs that the church holds. Taken together, the four layers of meanings in the medieval interpretation of Scripture gave people the literal and spiritual messages of the Bible, offering not only guidance to people on how they must live here on earth but also future hope of the resurrection and the second coming of Christ.

Calvin's insistence that we only read the Bible based on the literal and historical meanings of the text is born of his disagreement with the way the medieval church expanded its interpretation of the Bible into something not fully in line with what the Bible says. But this does not mean that Calvin rejects the allegorical, tropological, and anagogical senses altogether. In fact, he allows and even uses allegorical interpretation, whenever it is necessary, as long as it is simple, useful for instruction, and consistent with the Old and New Testaments. On this last point, Calvin emphasizes that Scripture should interpret Scripture. In other words, one should find the meaning of a particular biblical passage based on what other parts of the Bible say about it. Most important, one must find the meaning of the Old Testament in the New Testament.

Calvin's theological works are expressions of what he thinks the Bible means. When you read the *Institutes,* you will find that Calvin bases all his statements and explanations on what he thinks the Bible says regarding that very topic. He intended the *Institutes* to be read alongside his Bible commentaries. In the *Institutes* he often engages in debates with his opponents as he explains his theological views based on his understanding of Scripture. You can see how the *Institutes* is polemical. In his Bible commentaries, however, Calvin avoids such polemics because there, he wants people to understand the true meaning of Scripture. Therefore, it is often necessary for modern readers to read Calvin's *Institutes* together with his Bible commentaries.

When my students read the *Institutes* for the first time, they are often surprised to discover how biblical the book is, because many of them thought it was just a dense theological book without much grounding in the Bible. In other words, my students find that Calvin does not depart from the Bible when he makes his doctrinal statements. Of course, these doctrinal statements are based on his interpretation of the Bible. But in interpreting the Bible, he is also careful to explain what it teaches. I also find that Calvin is consistent in his interpretation, and that his interpretation is grounded on his firm conviction that he is trying to explain the very Word of God to the people. Calvin's whole theological system, therefore, is a system of biblical teaching that he develops systematically. At its core, Calvin's theology is his careful explication of the Bible written as a detailed elaboration of topics; together these form a strong foundation for what the church should believe. A theological methodology such as this is still important today. When we try to understand a certain theological or doctrinal belief, we need to start with a careful reading of the Bible, and then analyze and evaluate the views of theologians or scholars who discuss that topic so we can formulate what we believe and hold for ourselves.

Calvin's* Institutes *among theological treatises of other Reformers. As a theological work, the *Institutes* was not unique. Other Reformers before Calvin had already published works in a similar vein. Philip Melanchthon, for instance, published his famous *Loci Communes*, or *Commonplaces*, in 1521. He provided explanations of Christian doctrines within each appropriate locus or place, and he expanded the doctrinal teaching of the Lutheran branch of the Reformation. Another example is Ulrich Zwingli's *Commentary on True and False Religion*, published in 1525. Zwingli compared and contrasted the teachings of the Church of Rome and that of the Protestants, with a goal to show that Rome was in the wrong and the Protestants were in the right. You can sense the polemics even in the title of this work.

Calvin intended the *Institutes* as a teaching tool for pastors and theologians, as well as for people who were preparing themselves to become church leaders. He wrote most editions of the book in Latin, the language of the learned. He wanted his readers to be well educated in the church's doctrines. Because the *Institutes* is grounded in the Bible, Calvin intended for the *Institutes* to lead readers to consult his Bible commentaries.

In the *Institutes* Calvin integrates his study of the classical philosophers, such as Plato, Cicero, and Aristotle, and early Christian authors, including Athanasius, Chrysostom, the Cappadocian Fathers, and most notably Augustine, into his own thoughts. He also closely interacts with many medieval theologians, with Anselm and Aquinas occupying important spots in some of his discussions. Throughout the *Institutes* he often refers to Peter Lombard's *Four Books of Sentences*, either as a point of reference or to express his disagreement with this famous medieval theologian. And true to the polemical nature of the work, Calvin rarely holds back from revealing the mistakes he perceived in the Church of Rome. He believed that the Roman Catholic Church had departed from the true teaching of the Bible and had exchanged it with superstition. His critiques of Rome cover a wide range of doctrinal and ecclesial practices, spanning from the church's doctrine of transubstantiation, the power of the Papacy, the five sacraments that Protestants do not affirm, the church's beliefs in sainthood, pilgrimage to holy places, and relics to the issues that Luther and earlier Reformers had attacked, such as the selling of indulgences, purgatory, and justification through good works.

Taken as a whole, the *Institutes* was Calvin's way of presenting a well-rounded theological teaching, grounded in the Bible, for the edification of the church leaders who, in turn, would educate the whole church. In it, Calvin interacts with vast numbers of authors and thinkers from classical philosophy to the Christian thinkers who lived up to his time. As we will see, the education that he received, informed by the spirit of humanism that shaped the era leading up to his lifetime, paved the way for him to write this book. Humanism's central theme of going back to the sources (in Latin, *ad fontes*) became the foundation of his study of ancient writers as well as the original languages of the Bible, Greek and Hebrew. It was also the common thread that bound him together with other Reformers of his time. In this way, Calvin engaged with the long-standing Christian tradition from the earliest history of Christianity to his time. Thus, while Calvin's theology is deeply rooted in Scripture, he did not read the Bible without consulting the writings and opinions of others. His interaction with Christian authors of all ages was a way to show the true meaning of confessing that Christians are part of one holy, catholic, and apostolic church. As he wrote the *Institutes*, he sought to stand in the company of believers of all ages in every place.

Calvin's Lasting Impact in the Global Church

As a sixteenth-century Reformer, Calvin brought significant changes to the church that he led in Geneva. Yet the changes and renewals he implemented in his time did not affect only that city or last only during his lifetime. They went far beyond the geographical boundaries of one city, or one country, or even one continent. Calvin's thoughts and church practices have impacted Christianity all over the world for almost five centuries.

Calvin was a second-generation Reformer. When you think about the Reformation of the sixteenth century, you might think right away of Martin Luther. And that's understandable. Luther initiated changes in the church, moving it away from the medieval theology and practices that he believed to be incorrect and unbiblical. While Luther wanted to change many things about the church, at the center of his disagreement with the church was the issue of justification, or salvation, by grace alone. The medieval church in which Luther grew up taught that we are saved by God's grace in Christ together with our good works. In addition, the church taught that God still required a temporal punishment for sins people had not confessed, sins that had not been pardoned by God through the authority of the church. And even after sins were confessed, the church insisted, God's justice had not been satisfied, and therefore people still needed to receive punishment. They would undergo this punishment in purgatory after they died. Remission of that punishment was made available by the church in the form of an *indulgence*. In practice, the church could issue a letter to a person to demonstrate a certain kind of penance. It later devised a plan that would allow people to bypass their time in purgatory if they purchased a letter that the church issued, called a "letter of indulgence." When people purchased a letter, depending on the sum of money they paid, they could secure complete freedom from purgatory. And even better, they could also purchase letters of indulgence for other people, such as their parents, who had died and were believed to be going through the fire of purgatory. Luther disagreed with the selling of the letter of indulgences because the practice diminished the significance of the death of Christ for our salvation and put at the center of our salvation "good works" in the form of purchasing the letter. Following the teaching of the Bible, Luther emphasized that salvation is only by the grace of God.

In this and other respects, Calvin continued Luther's work. The two didn't agree on every point, but in his teachings Calvin, like Luther before him, consistently argued that we are only saved by God's grace. We can do nothing to earn our own salvation. But Calvin did not stop with making changes in the theological teaching of the church. He developed an extensive plan to implement the changes. The first step he took was to insist on people's knowledge of the teaching of Scripture. Still in the footsteps of Luther, Calvin wanted people to worship, hear the Bible and sermons, say their prayers, and recite their creed all in their own mother tongue. Luther had started this by translating the Bible into German. Before Luther, Latin was the language of the Western church. You can easily imagine that ordinary people living in Germany who only spoke German would not have had a clue what the priests said at Mass. Before the Reformation, people went to church not to understand the message of the Bible but only to receive the Eucharist, which would later amount to the grace of God, or salvation. While there was beautiful music in the church, the choir sang in Latin, so ordinary people did not actively participate in the singing. They were there only to partake of the Eucharist.

Calvin wanted the people in Geneva to hear sermons in French so that they could understand them well. In addition, he wanted people to sing the psalms, recite the Apostles' Creed, and pray the Lord's Prayer in French. He intended that all these participatory activities at church should be integral parts of worship that would build people's understanding of God, themselves, and their relationship with God. Therefore, in matters concerning worship, Calvin worked hard to ensure that people gained knowledge of God by regularly going to church. He developed an easy way for the church in Geneva to sing the psalms, putting the texts into metrical form in the familiar language. Calvin's insistence on including the congregation in singing at church is one of the lasting influences of Calvin on the church all these years later. Calvin was not the only Reformer who sought to change how the church worshiped, but his emphases upon hearing God's Word and singing the psalms have deeply informed the church to this day.

Figure 1.2. The Reformation Wall in Geneva featuring (from left) William Farel, John Calvin, Theodore Beza, and John Knox

The Reformation of the church that took place under Calvin in Geneva was not just about theological doctrine and worship in the church. It was also intended to reform people's lives. To ensure this, Calvin insisted on church discipline, which was upheld by a body called the Consistory, consisting of all the ministers of the church in Geneva and twelve councilors from the different councils of the city. I will discuss the Consistory later in this book. At this point, I just want to underline that as a leader, Calvin wanted to ensure that people became followers of Christ who would know the teaching of the Bible and live accordingly. The Consistory was there to ensure that the people did both. While it is perhaps understandable that Calvin had to take such an approach in maintaining discipline, it is also understandable that people did not like such strict discipline. In subsequent years and even centuries, the Consistory has received a bad reputation. However, Calvin's insistence on discipline has had a lasting impact on Christians all over the world by showing how Christian faith must be reflected in daily living.

Another important aspect of Calvin's influence concerned the understanding of marriage and the place of children in the church. Before the Reformation, the way people got married was much different than it is today. In medieval Europe, a man and a woman could go together to a tavern, drink in the name of marriage in the presence of witnesses or promise to be married to each other, and right away they would be considered married.[3] Then they would engage in a sexual relationship right after the promise of marriage. Of course, this practice led to a variety of problems. First, it would be rather difficult to make a distinction between a promise to be married and social drinking at taverns. One party, either the man or the woman, might easily deny that they intended to be married when they drank together. Most often it was the men who would deny that a marriage took place, but there were cases when the women denied that they had the intention to be married when they drank with the other party. Another problem that often arose was the practice of polygamy. Let's imagine a man whose line of work required him to travel from one town to another. He might get married in one town then repeat the act in another. In those days communication between people living in different towns was not as easy as it is today. Therefore, people—most likely men—could potentially be married multiple times in different places. To prevent this from happening, the church in Geneva developed a new practice. The church order of 1541 contained a regulation that couples should be married at church, that the ceremony should take place on a day when there was a church service, and that

---

[3]For further discussion on this issue, see, for instance, John Witt Jr. and Robert M. Kingdon, *Sex, Marriage, and Family in John Calvin's Geneva*, vol. 1, *Courtship, Engagement, and Marriage* (Grand Rapids, MI: Eerdmans, 2006).

the couple's intention to marry should be announced prior to the intended day of their wedding. This practice, called the marriage banns, became standard. Interestingly, if you go to Indonesia today, you will still find similar practices in many of the churches of various theological persuasions, including Reformed, Presbyterian, Baptist, Methodist, and many others.

Children were an important feature of Calvin's ministry and theology. He believed that children should receive instruction in the faith while still young. One good way of teaching children is through singing. The church order published in Geneva in 1541, which provided guidance on how the church should operate there, states that the little children should be taught how to sing the psalms. Even though Calvin's name is not written as the author of the church order, I believe Calvin was primarily behind its publication. The church order implies that by teaching young children to sing the psalms, the church could be sure that when the children grow up, they will carry with them the knowledge of God and his words. When the church teaches children to sing, these children will go home and sing the psalms there. As they do, their parents will hear the psalms in French, and they will learn too. What a marvelous idea! Calvin was empowering the children to teach their parents.

The parents of these children were born and raised in the medieval church, where they did not participate in worship, did not receive enough teaching of the Bible, were not accustomed to hearing sermons in their own language, and did not recite the creed and pray in their mother tongue. It was hard for these parents and adults to undergo change as they joined the Reformed church even before Calvin arrived in Geneva in 1536. These adults needed more time to adjust themselves and to embrace the newness that the Reformation brought. But the children were different. Many of them were born after the Reformation. Therefore, they started their

Christian lives already in the context of the new church. In Geneva, the children in the Latin school received instruction on psalm singing from a precentor every day. The children in turn led the congregational singing at worship services, under the guidance of the precentor. By empowering the children to sing and to bring the message of the psalms home, Calvin effectively helped the adults transition into the new church.

Still fixing his eyes on the young children, Calvin thought very hard about giving them further instruction in the faith. To that end, he wrote and published several catechisms during his lifetime. Catechisms did not originate with Calvin. Long before the Reformation, the early and medieval churches had used catechisms or catechetical materials. Before Calvin's time, Luther had already published his *Small Catechism* in 1529 as a way to help parents teach the rudiments of the Christian faith to their children at home. Calvin took another step by using the catechism as a link between baptism and the Lord's Supper, the two sacraments of the Protestant churches. As was the common church practice in the day among both the majority of the Protestant churches and the Roman Catholic Church, Calvin's church in Geneva baptized infants. As these baptized children grew, they needed instruction to help them understand the teaching of the Bible. These youngsters were not allowed to partake in the Lord's Supper before they made their profession of faith when they were old enough to understand. These children had to go through catechism classes that the church held every Sunday at noon. The catechism books that Calvin published were the material used to instruct the young people. I'm sure some of my readers will have also been through catechism classes at church. And even if you did not have that experience, I hope you will agree with me that faith formation of children is important and that the church must take an active role in educating the young. This is another one of Calvin's lasting influences in the church.

People often think of Calvin as a dour, stern, and cold theologian who only thought about doctrines. However, I find him to be a warm pastor who cared deeply about God's people and whose influence on his own tradition and the global church is undeniable. I hope in the next chapters you will meet a man who loved God deeply and who did all that he could to ensure that people would get to know God intimately, worship him with all their hearts, and live as Christians who glorify God all the days of their lives.

Suggestions for Further Reading

Backus, Irena, and Philip Benedict. *Calvin and his Influence 1509–2009*. New York: Oxford University Press, 2011.

Gordon, Bruce. *Calvin*. New Haven, CT: Yale University Press, 2009.

Holder, R. Ward, ed. *John Calvin in Context*. New York: Cambridge University Press, 2019.

Kingdon, Robert, Thomas A. Lambert, and Isabella M. Watts, eds. *Registers of the Consistory of Geneva in the Time of Calvin*. Trans. M. Wallace McDonald. Vol. 1, *1542–1544*. Grand Rapids, MI: Eerdmans, 2000.

Muller, Richard. *The Unaccommodated Calvin*. New York: Oxford University Press, 2000.

Partee, Richard. *The Theology of John Calvin*. Louisville, KY: Westminster John Knox Press, 2008.

Steinmetz, David. *Calvin in Context*. 2nd ed. New York: Oxford University Press, 2010.

Who Was John Calvin?

Early Life and Education

In the Indonesian language, my mother tongue, there is a saying whose English translation roughly means, "If you don't know a person, you cannot love them." The implication behind this saying is that loving or understanding people requires taking the first step and making the effort to get to know them. But once we know them, we can love them quite well. In this chapter, I intend to write a brief overview of Calvin's life so that you can know him better. I hope that by learning about his life, journey, and struggles you will grow in your understanding of his theology, thoughts, and work. I do not mean this chapter to be a comprehensive biography of Calvin. There are many good biographies available today. I encourage you to pick one up if you want to get a detailed view of Calvin's life.[1] But I have chosen here to follow primarily a biography written by Theodore Beza, one of Calvin's contemporaries.[2] As a sketch, this chapter will take us through the important events of Calvin's life to aid you in knowing his life journey.

---

[1]Among the more recent and extremely well written biographies of Calvin is Bruce Gordon, *Calvin* (New Haven, CT: Yale University Press, 2009). See the "For Further Reading" section for additional suggestions.

[2]There are many editions of Beza's *Life of Calvin* available in English today. One is included in John Calvin, *Tracts and Treatises on the Reformation of the Church*, trans. Henry Beveridge (Grand Rapids, MI: Eerdmans, 1958).

Calvin was born on July 10, 1509. This means that when Martin Luther wrote his Ninety-Five Theses and nailed them to the door of the Castle Church in Wittenberg on October 31, 1517, Calvin was only eight years old. His birthplace was a small town called Noyon in the region of Picardy in northern France, about sixty miles north of Paris. He was a true Frenchman, and he loved his native land and its people dearly all his life. In writing his books, especially the *Institutes*, he had his fellow French constantly in mind. He even dedicated the *Institutes* to King Francis I of France, defending the case of those in France who were persecuted because they followed the beliefs of the "Evangelicals"—a term that, at the time, applied to the people who moved away from the Roman Catholic Church and embraced the beliefs of the Reformation.

Calvin's given name was Jean Cauvin. His father was Gerard Cauvin, a well-respected man in town who worked for Bishop Charles de Hangest performing administrative duties for the cathedral chapter, the assembly of clerics who advised the bishop. Gerard was originally from a nearby city of Pont-l'Evèque but then moved to Noyon in 1479. He married Jeanne Lefranc in 1497, and together the couple had four sons: Charles, Jean, Antoine, and François, who died when he was young. Calvin's mother died when he was still a boy. His father remarried and from his second marriage had two daughters, Marie and another whose name was never recorded anywhere. When he was still at home in Noyon, Calvin went to a school for boys at the Collège des Capettes.

In the spring of 1521, Calvin was sent to live and study together with the children of the Montmorts, relatives of Bishop Charles de Hangest, the employer of Calvin's father. They were a family of noble birth. Calvin's father had intended Jean to be a priest, and the education he received with the children of the Montmorts was the first step toward that goal. Bishop de Hangest arranged for him to get some funding, called a church benefice, from the Chapel of La

Gèsine. His task was to serve at the altar of Gèsine, in the cathedral of Noyon. This job was suitable for his preparation to be a priest, and it gave him an early experience of working in the church.

After about two years living with the Montmorts, Calvin went to study in Paris along with two of the sons of the Montmorts. They attended the Collège de la Marche. There he studied under a Latin professor, Mathurin Cordier. The relationship with Cordier lasted for a long time. Later, in 1536, when Calvin lived in Geneva, he invited his former teacher to the city. When the Geneva Academy was officially opened in 1559, Calvin offered Cordier a position to teach in the academy. While still a student in Paris, Calvin changed his French name into its Latin form, Ioannis Calvinus, which has been Anglicized into John Calvin. However, Calvin and the two sons of the Montmorts only stayed at la Marche for a few months. They soon moved to study at a different school in Paris, Collège de Montaigu, where Calvin studied under a Spanish tutor, Antonio Coronel, whose teaching focused on the philosophies of Aristotle, Plato, Stoicism, and Epicureanism. There he learned the scholastic method of education under which students studied the seven liberal arts. This curriculum centered on the study of three subjects called the *trivium*: grammar, rhetoric, and logic. Once the students mastered them, they moved up to the four subjects called the *quadrivium*: arithmetic, geometry, music, and astronomy. The Collège de Montaigu was greatly influenced by the Brethren of the Common Life, which emphasized the life of piety to its students. It was there that Calvin may have been exposed to the new way of devotion, the *devotio moderna*, popularized by Thomas à Kempis in his book *The Imitation of Christ*.

In September 1527, Calvin received another benefice (financial support) from the church of Saint-Martin-de-Martheville, a small village located not far from Noyon. However, about the same time, Calvin's father changed his mind regarding his plan for his son's future, wanting Jean to become a lawyer rather than spend his life in the priesthood. Later in his life, when he wrote the preface to his commentary on the book of Psalms in 1557, Calvin reflected that his father thought a profession as a lawyer would give him a life of prosperity. Modern scholars, however, think that the main reason for Gerard Cauvin's change of heart was a dispute with the Noyon cathedral chapter over the issue of property settlement, which eventually led to Gerard's excommunication from the church in 1531. Whatever the exact circumstances, Calvin followed his father's wish and moved to Orléans.

At Orléans, he studied under a famous law teacher, Pierre de l'Estoile, a French lawyer. Calvin flourished in his study of law. Because of Calvin's excellent academic achievements, L'Estoile treated him more as a colleague than a student. In Orléans, Calvin also studied under Melchior Wolmar, a teacher of Greek from Germany who was very much persuaded by Luther's thoughts and teachings. Another important contact made during this time was Pierre Robert Olivetan, a cousin who was well versed in Scripture. Olivetan encouraged Calvin to study the Bible deeply and to reject the unbiblical beliefs of the Church of Rome.

In the spring of 1529, Calvin moved to the University of Bourges. There he studied under an Italian teacher, Andrea Alciati, a scholar who was famous for his work analyzing the *Corpus Juris,* a large collection of documents regarding the law used in the medieval era. Alciati was invited to teach at Bourges through the influence of Marguerite of Angoulême, a patroness of the university. She was the sister of King Francis I and later became Queen of Navarre through her second marriage. As the queen, she made great efforts to protect the Huguenots, the followers of the Reformed beliefs in France, efforts likely influenced by her previous correspondence with Calvin. At that time, Wolmar, his professor from Orléans, also moved to Bourges. According to Beza, Wolmar was Calvin's most beloved teacher. He expressed his great respect for Wolmar when he dedicated his commentary on 2 Corinthians to his former teacher.

Calvin later attended Collège Royal in Paris, and he was deeply involved in the circles of the French humanism that shaped his thoughts. He got to know humanist scholar Jacques Lefèvre d'Étaples, whose approach influenced him. Quite possibly, Calvin first studied Hebrew at the Collège Royal. In April 1530 a controversy erupted at the Sorbonne (later, the University of Paris) due to the publication of a document called *Determinatio facultatis,* in which the faculty of the Collège Royal received harsh words because of their support of the humanist method of scholarly biblical interpretation. King Francis I had founded the college earlier that year, and the rector was Guillaume Budé, a humanist. The Sorbonne was a strong supporter of the Church of Rome, and it suspected that the faculty who wrote the document were Lutherans.

> Humanism was a movement that started in Italy in the fourteenth century and reached its highest point in the fifteenth century. From Italy it spread throughout Europe. As a major intellectual movement, it sought to go back to the sources of classical studies of ancient Greece and Rome. It became one of the driving forces behind the Reformation in the sixteenth century, as Reformers such as Luther, Zwingli, Calvin, and others received their training in humanism. Carrying on the spirit of humanism, they read the Bible in its original languages of Hebrew and Greek instead of just reading it in Latin, and therefore opened new learning beyond what the Church of Rome provided the people at that time.

Calvin's father died on May 26, 1531. Calvin traveled back to Noyon for his father's funeral. Charles, his older brother, was able to negotiate for a church burial for their father, even though he had been excommunicated by the church. After the death of his father, Calvin returned to Paris and abandoned his study of law, though the skills that he developed in that field would benefit him throughout his life. In Paris he was back in the circle of humanism and, using his own money, he published his first book, a commentary on a treatise by Seneca, *De Clementia*, in 1532. Around this time Calvin likely abandoned his adherence to the Church of Rome and followed the spirit and beliefs of the Protestant Reformation. We do not know the exact time and circumstances of this change. In the preface to the commentary of the book of Psalms, he only states that he had a "sudden conversion" and that God had brought him to a "teachable mind" in true godliness.[3]

Calvin became a good friend of Nicolas Cop, the rector of the University of Paris. At the opening ceremony of the new academic year of the university on November 1, 1533 (All Saints' Day), Cop made a speech that was very much in line with the views and beliefs of the Evangelicals, or Protestants. He spoke about the relationship between law and gospel that stood at the center of Martin Luther's theology. This speech put Cop in a difficult position against other administrators and faculty members of the university, who did not embrace Protestant views, which were still illegal. The faculty of the Sorbonne made a formal complaint against Cop to the Parlement of Paris. Cop fled the city to Basel before he was formally charged. We have reason to believe that Calvin had a part in writing Cop's address before the university, and he too fled Paris in haste before the authorities arrested him.

Calvin moved to the province of Saintonge in the southern region of France, where he assumed the pseudonym Charles d'Espeville and lived in the house of Louis du Tillet. Here he started

---

[3]John Calvin, *Commentary on the Book of Psalms* (Edinburgh: Calvin Translation Society, 1845), 1:xl.

to write the first edition of what would become the *Institutes*. While living in Saintonge, he went to Nérac to visit his former teacher Lefèvre d'Étaples, who by then was quite old and who had moved to that region because he had also faced persecution at the Sorbonne. Calvin left Saintonge to return to Paris, still using his pseudonym. There he encountered Michael Servetus, a man whose unorthodox views of the Trinity would later stir controversy in Geneva and in Calvin's life.

Between 1533 and 1534, Calvin made several trips around France, including into Paris. In October 1534, a controversy on the Eucharist erupted when placards, or fliers, containing harsh criticism against the way the sacrament was celebrated by the Church of Rome were found all over Paris. One was reportedly posted even on the door of the king's bedroom. Later on, these placards were also found all over France. The author behind the placards was believed to be Antoine Marcourt, a minister in Neuchatel. The king was not pleased with the Protestants, and he made an edict against the "Lutherans." Several hundred people were arrested, and many were executed. The situation in France became too dangerous for Calvin. He and du Tillet left France for Basel, making a short stop in Strasbourg. At this time, Basel was a center of humanist scholarship and publishing, and some of the important thinkers of the day lived there, including Cop, Johannes Oecolampadius, Wolfgang Capito, Heinrich Bullinger, Pierre Viret, and Guillaume Farel. Calvin started to build close relationships with these people, many of whom provided support for and worked with Calvin for the remainder of his life in his work as a church leader and Reformer.

While in Basel, Calvin continued his studies of biblical languages. He took Hebrew classes taught by Sebastian Munster, and he continued his study of Greek, now under Simon Grynaeus. In June 1535, Robert Olivetan, Calvin's cousin, published a French translation of the Bible. Calvin wrote the foreword to this publication in Latin.

During this time, he completed the first edition of the *Institutes*, which he dedicated to King Francis I, dated August 23, 1535. The first edition of *Institutes of the Christian Religion* was published in Basel in 1536.

Just before the *Institutes* was published, Calvin traveled to Italy together with du Tillet. They stayed in the city of Ferrara, and they encountered several significant supporters of the Protestant movement, including Renée of France, the daughter of King Louis XII and sister-in-law of Francis I, who by then had married Hercule d'Este, Duke of Ferrara, making her the Duchess of Ferrara. Among the most important connections Calvin made while in town was Clement Marot, a French poet. When Calvin served the Reformed church in Geneva later in his life, he worked closely with Marot to write and publish the metrical psalms, which were the only canticles sung in the church in Geneva. Calvin and du Tillet returned to Basel after they learned that Charles V, the Emperor of the Holy Roman Empire, had pressured Duke Hercule d'Este, who was not in favor of Protestantism, to ask the guests to leave Ferrara.

After staying in Basel for a short time, Calvin went back to France. At that point, the country had issued a temporary amnesty toward the Protestants, allowing them to return to France with a requirement that within six months they must renounce their adherence to Protestantism. Calvin went to Paris to meet with old friends and to settle some unfinished matters because he believed—rightly—that after the amnesty ended, he would not be able to remain in his homeland. His younger brother Antoine and half sister Marie accompanied him when he left Paris. His intention was to go to Strasbourg to live and pursue a quiet life of writing. When Calvin and his companions set out for Strasbourg, however, there was a war between Charles V and Francis I, so they had to make a detour through Geneva and wait for the troops that blocked the road to leave the following day. Calvin's plan was to stay just overnight in

Geneva. As so often happens in the history of the church, things turned out quite differently than planned.

In Geneva: The First Time

Geneva was an exciting place in the sixteenth century. Earlier, it had been under the control of the Duchy of Savoy, but in 1526 it gained independence from Savoy and aligned itself with Bern and Fribourg, two Swiss cantons or regions. This alliance was based on an agreement that if one of them was in trouble, the other two would provide help. The Bishop of Geneva, however, was friendly with Savoy because he needed its support. Understandably, he wanted the city to be restored to its original arrangement under the Duke of Savoy. However, Bern, which had become Protestant in 1528, had tried to turn Geneva into a Protestant town by supporting Guillaume Farel and his assistants in bringing the Reformation to the city. Because of the support from Bern, Geneva was able to break away from the Bishop of Geneva and the Duke of Savoy. Under Farel's leadership, the people of Geneva took an oath to embrace the Reformation on May 21, 1536. That is, Geneva had approved the Reformation prior to Calvin's arrival.

Du Tillet was already in Geneva when Calvin passed through the city to stay overnight. He notified Farel, who had been a minister in Geneva, that Calvin was in town. Without wasting much time, Farel talked to Calvin and strongly urged him to stay in Geneva to help him further the work of the Reformation there. The experienced minister was forceful in getting Calvin to stay in Geneva. In 1557, in his preface to the commentary on the book of Psalms, Calvin recalled how he felt when Farel pleaded with him to stay in Geneva. This is how he recalled the interaction with Farel:

> And after having learned that my heart was set upon devoting myself to private studies, for which I wished to keep myself

free from other pursuits, and finding that he gained nothing by entreaties, he proceeded to utter an imprecation that God would curse my retirement, and the tranquility of the studies which I sought, if I should withdraw and refuse to give assistance, when the necessity was so urgent. By this imprecation I was so stricken with terror, that I desisted from the journey which I had undertaken, but sensible of my natural bashfulness and timidity, I would not bring myself under obligation to discharge any particular office.[4]

Calvin started his ministry in Geneva as a teacher at the church, lecturing on Paul's letter to the Romans. Shortly thereafter, in August 1536, he was appointed a professor of sacred literature. Around that time, Geneva and Bern formed a strong alliance, and Protestantism grew stronger in both places. At the same time, Lausanne also embraced Protestantism. A few months afterward, Calvin, Farel, and Pierre Viret went to Lausanne, where they participated in a theological debate. Calvin made a favorable impression on those who attended, demonstrating a depth of theological knowledge, especially regarding the theology of the church fathers.

In Geneva, Calvin took up the work of reforming the church. He saw that the young Protestant church in Geneva needed clear guidance in conducting its services and giving direction for the people to live as Christians, so the first steps he took were to draft a church order and a short confession of faith for the church. The church order included a catechism and instructions for both church discipline and worship, including how people should sing at church services and how frequently they should celebrate the Lord's Supper.

Calvin and Farel presented the documents to the Small Council and the Council of Two Hundred, the governing bodies of the city

---

[4]Calvin, "Preface," in *Commentary on the Psalms,* 1:xl-xli.

of Geneva, in late 1536 or early 1537. But Calvin encountered a rocky path toward the councils' acceptance of the standards he wanted to use for Christians in the city. The Genevan city council did not want to accept a weekly celebration of the Lord's Supper as Calvin had proposed. They decided to hold the sacraments quarterly. The approval of the confession of faith was delayed several months until July 1537. Many of Geneva's inhabitants refused to subscribe to it, so Calvin and Farel prevented those who had not subscribed to it from partaking in the Lord's Supper. Some of these people were Anabaptists, and the tension between Calvin and the Anabaptists escalated.

The Anabaptist movement had begun in Zurich. The movement sought to separate as far as possible not just from the theology and the practices of the Church of Rome but also from government and society in general. Those who followed is principles, including Felix Manz, Conrad Grebel, George Blaurock, and Balthasar Hubmaier, are often considered to be part of the Radical Reformation. Its fundamental conviction was that Christians should separate themselves from society to form a new society based solely on the teaching of Scripture. The movement was called "Anabaptist," which means to "baptize again," because one of its main principles was rejecting infant baptism. Instead, the founders of this movement, in their visible protest and rejection of established church practices, baptized each other as adults. The Anabaptists rejected society and culture outside their community because they considered them to be sinful, but such beliefs and practices—rejecting infant baptism and refusing to take oaths or to participate in the military—put them squarely at odds with both Roman Catholics and other Protestants and led many civil leaders to regard them as rebellious or seditious. Indeed, the Anabaptists faced persecution at the hands of fellow Christians, and sadly they were sometimes killed, often by drowning. The Anabaptists became a regular opponent in

Calvin's works because he wanted to distinguish his reforming efforts from the views of the Anabaptists.

Calvin also faced challenges from individuals who opposed his theological stance and ecclesial practices. For example, Pierre Caroli challenged him on his view of the Trinity. Caroli went about calling Calvin and Farel heretics who embraced the teaching of Arianism, a classical heresy that rejected the full divinity of Christ, because Farel did not use the terms *Trinity* and *persons* in his writing.[5] In reply to Caroli, Calvin stated that he and Farel did not reject the terms at all. In fact, in the 1536 edition of the *Institutes* he strongly defended the credal statement on the Trinity.

In February 1538, Geneva elected four new syndics, the four men who held the highest leadership position in the city. These four syndics leaned significantly toward Bern, and they did not agree with Calvin and Farel on many significant issues. The syndics wanted Calvin and Farel to conduct worship services the same way the churches in Bern did. They also instructed all churches in Geneva to follow the liturgy of the Bernese churches. The disagreement between the syndics and the two ministers eventually ended in the expulsion of Calvin and Farel from Geneva on April 23, 1538. Calvin and Farel left the city and went to Basel by way of Bern and Zurich. In Basel, Calvin stayed with his former Greek teacher and friend, Simon Grynaeus. Calvin had sought to bring great reform to Geneva, but the future of his life in ministry was, at this point, uncertain.

---

[5]Arianism was a heresy in the fourth century promoted by Arius. Arius rejected the divine nature of Christ because he believed that only God the Father was God and that Jesus was not eternal like the Father, but rather he was a creature. Arius infamously spread the statement "there was time when he was not" to refer to Jesus, who, according to this view, was not the eternally begotten of the Father and therefore was a created being. The Council of Nicea in AD 325 declared Arius a heretic and articulated the first version of what we now call the Nicene Creed. That creed has become a standard of orthodoxy ever since, and it clearly states that Jesus the Son is of the same substance as the Father and therefore eternally divine.

In Strasbourg

Martin Bucer, who was ministering in Strasbourg, invited Calvin to come and serve the church there. A large community of French Protestant refugees had settled in the city, and Bucer thought that Calvin, a refugee himself, could serve the people. Calvin accepted the invitation. Strasbourg was an ideal place for him, and he enjoyed serving God's people there. You might say that Calvin became a proper minister during his time in Strasbourg. He spent a significant amount of time thinking about the liturgy and worship. He also taught New Testament at the preparatory school. He learned from Bucer how to conduct and apply church discipline, and he also sharpened his skills in preaching and pastoral care. He became a faithful shepherd for the French refugees in Strasbourg. Furthermore, he developed the idea of singing the metrical psalms in French, which would become one of Calvin's signature impacts in reforming the church.

During this period, Calvin also revised and enlarged his *Institutes*, and a second edition was published in 1539. That same year he published a commentary on Paul's letter to the Romans as well as a short treatise regarding the Lord's Supper. The Lord's Supper had been a contentious issue both between Protestants and Catholics as well as among Protestants. Famously, Luther and Zwingli had a sharp disagreement on the question of Christ's presence in the Lord's Supper, which they were never able to resolve. Calvin's intention in writing the treatise was to reach out to the Lutherans on matters regarding the sacrament. He wanted to build a bridge with them and mend the relationship broken with his earlier criticism of the Lutheran position. While he was ministering in Strasbourg, he traveled to Frankfurt to meet with Philip Melanchthon, Luther's successor, to discuss the doctrine. Prior to the meeting, he sent his German colleague the articles on the Lord's Supper that he had written as a starting point of their conversation. Melanchthon seemed appreciative of Calvin's view, and at that point he considered unity between the German and Swiss churches possible.

Calvin disagreed with Zwingli's position that the Lord's Supper is primarily a remembrance of what Christ has done for the salvation of humanity. Zwingli rejected the view that Christ is present physically in the bread and wine of the Lord's Supper because Christ's body is in heaven. He emphasized that the bread and the wine are the signs that signify Christ. He further argued that, while we distinguish the signs and the actual thing they signify, the wine and bread of the Lord's Supper actually represent Christ's sacrificial death for his people. Therefore, while Christ's body is in heaven, Christ's spirit still takes center stage on earth. But Zwingli also disagreed with Luther's view, which affirmed the physical presence of the body and blood of Christ together with the bread and wine in the sacrament. Luther's view of the bodily presence of Jesus in the Lord's Supper is still quite close to that of the view of the Church of Rome; namely, both affirm Christ's bodily or corporeal presence. The difference is that Rome believes that the substance of the bread and the wine changes into the body and the blood of Jesus (a view known as *transubstantiation*), while Luther thought that the body and the blood of Jesus are together with the bread and wine (a view known as "real presence" or *consubstantiation*). Theological disagreements regarding this sacrament continued even after Calvin left Strasbourg. Toward the end of Luther's life, the older Reformer became more critical of the positions of other Reformers, including those of Bucer, Bullinger, and Calvin. In September 1544 Luther published his *Short Confession of the Holy Sacrament* to reaffirm where he stood on the matter against the churches in Switzerland. Even though theologically he disagreed with Luther, Calvin still showed respect and appreciation for him. In a letter to Bullinger he called Luther an eminent Christian who was endowed with gifts.

Most important, Calvin reminded Bullinger, Luther had spread the true doctrine of salvation and remained a faithful servant of God.[6]

Calvin called on the connection previously made with Melanchthon, when he had met with him in Frankfurt, in an attempt to reach out to Luther to find some support for the French Evangelicals, especially on a problem called Nicodemism. Some Evangelicals in France did not leave the Church of Rome for fear of persecution. These people were called the Nicodemites, a term based on the story of Nicodemus, a Pharisee who met secretly with Jesus at night (Jn 3:1-15). Calvin needed Luther's words for these Nicodemites, and he attempted to contact Luther through Philip Melanchthon. In January 1545, Calvin wrote Melanchthon two letters. One was for Melanchthon himself, in which he stated that he valued his friendship, and that friendship did not mean that they had to agree on every view. The second was for Luther, and he asked Melanchthon to judge whether he would give the letter to Luther. In this letter, he asked Luther not to hold his disagreement with him as a hindrance to support the French churches. Melanchthon never gave Calvin's letter to Luther because he knew that his older colleague disagreed with Calvin, who he placed in the same group as the Zwinglians. Calvin was disappointed that he heard nothing back from Germany, but it did not stop his efforts to unify the Protestant cause.

When he was in Strasbourg, Calvin also met Jean Stordeur, a former Anabaptist from Liege who later joined the French refugees. At the time, Stordeur was married to Idelette de Bure, and they had two children, one boy and one girl, Charles and Judith. By the time Stordeur died of the plague in 1540, Calvin had already received some pressure to get married, with his brother Antoine, Bucer, and Farel all attempting to play matchmaker for him with no success. A

---

[6]Calvin wrote this letter in November 1544. See John Calvin, Letter CXXII, in *Letters of John Calvin*, ed. Jules Bonnet (New York: B. Franklin, 1973), 1:433.

year after Stordeur died, Calvin married Idelette and then adopted Idelette's two children as his own.

Even while serving the church in Strasbourg, Calvin never took his attention away from the Christians in Geneva. The Genevan church continued to face troubles that stemmed from the tension between the church and the city leaders, but it retained many strong supporters, including Calvin and Farel. This group, which included Antoine Saunier and Mathurin Cordier, Calvin's former teacher, were called the Guillermins after Farel's French first name, Guillaume. The opposition group against the Guillermins was called the Articulants, who had appointed ministers when Calvin and Farel were deposed from the city. Understandably, the Guillermins refused to support them. From Strasbourg, Calvin urged his followers in Geneva not to create a schism within the church. He wanted them to accept one another so that they could continue partaking in the Lord's Supper and worshiping peacefully together. But it was not easy to unite these two groups. On Christmas Day 1538, the church in Geneva celebrated the Lord's Supper, but Saunier and his followers did not participate. In response, the city council banished the Guillermins from the city. But the problem in Geneva went beyond this issue. When matters got complicated and the relationship between the church and the Geneva city council became difficult to handle, the ministers requested that the city council release them from their duties. Geneva sought help from Bern. The ministers from Bern met with their Genevan counterparts to discuss the matter in the city of Morges on March 12, 1539. Finally, they came to an agreement that the Genevan ministers would take care of the matter following close consultation with the banished ministers. When Calvin received the news, he was delighted that there was a reconciliation in the church in Geneva. But the matter was not resolved.

Cardinal Jacopo Sadoleto, bishop of Carpentras, took the helm in efforts by the Church of Rome to win the city of Geneva back. On March 8, 1539, Sadoleto wrote a letter to Geneva, attempting to persuade the Genevans to return to Rome. Because nobody in Geneva felt adequate to reply to the letter, the church turned to someone they knew could offer a response, even though they had previously expelled him from the city. Calvin replied to Sadoleto on September 1 of that year. In the letter, Calvin explained to Sadoleto that the Reformation was a movement of following God's Word. The Protestants were not destroying the church, he argued, but renewing and restoring it. Sadoleto's letter and Calvin's reply were published in Strasbourg, and a year later the city council of Geneva released them to be published in both Latin and French so that the people in Geneva were able to read them.

The Genevans wanted Calvin to return to lead the church there. Calvin's friends, including Cordier and Viret, also urged him to return. In a letter to Farel, Calvin wrote that, even though he loved the people of Geneva, he still harbored the memories of how badly they had treated him the first time he was there. In addition, he also thought that God had already given him a flourishing ministry serving the French refugees in Strasbourg. He felt torn between the two cities, but he stated that, even though he may not decide to return to Geneva voluntarily, he was willing to listen to the voices of others. On October 13, 1540, the Geneva city council sent a formal letter to invite Calvin to return. He did not respond to the letter for two days. He openly told the Genevans his dilemma. On the one hand, he was convinced that a minister should remain where God has placed him, but on the other hand, he also wanted to listen to the call and the need of the church in Geneva. On October 27, Calvin wrote to Farel again, stating that, if it was up to him, he would not follow Farel's advice to return to Geneva. However, because he regarded himself not as his own master but rather a servant of God, he willingly offered his heart promptly and sincerely as a true sacrifice to the Lord.[7] This statement and the depiction of a heart on an open hand has become an emblem of Calvin's life and ministry.[8]

FUN FACT

The official seals of Calvin Theological Seminary, my alma mater, and Calvin University bear the picture of a hand and a heart with a Latin inscription surrounding them: *Cor meum tibi offero Domine, prompte et sincere*, which means: "My heart I offer to you, Lord, promptly and sincerely." This seal reflects Calvin's statement to Farel regarding his return to Geneva. Beginning in the 1540s, Calvin used the image of a hand and a heart as a seal for his letters.

Calvin discussed the letter from Geneva with the ministers in Strasbourg. Bucer finally agreed that it would be good for Calvin to return to Geneva. In the interim, the church sent Viret from Lausanne to go to Geneva and lead the church there. At long last, Calvin's return was made possible when on May 1, 1541, the city council of Geneva issued a formal statement revoking the ban on Calvin, and the people of Geneva recalled him to the city. Calvin found himself back in the city on September 13, 1541.

In Geneva: The Second Time

Spiritual and civil organization. The first step Calvin took in continuing his work to reform the church in Geneva was to write a draft of a church order that would regulate worship and church ministry

---

[7]Calvin, Letter LIV, in *Letters of John Calvin*, 1:210-14.
[8]Calvin's statement of offering his heart to the Lord "promptly and sincerely" comes from his letter to Farel in August 1541. See Letter LXXIII, in *Letters of John Calvin*, 1:280-81.

as well as ensuring that Christian conduct would be maintained in the city. A group of people consisting of Calvin, six members of the Genevan city council, and four other ministers worked on the draft of the new church order. They worked very fast, and the committee presented the draft to the full city council on September 26, 1541. In November of that same year, the city council approved the new church order, which is called *Les ordinnances ecclesiastique* in French, or the Ecclesiastical Ordinances. Even though Calvin did not get everything he wanted in the church order, it reflected much of what he wished for reformation of the church in Geneva.[9]

On the same day that the church order was officially approved, Calvin and two others were appointed to work on revising the legislation in Geneva, though their revisions largely followed what Geneva previously had in place. Knowing a bit about the political dynamics of the city will help you understand the context of Calvin's ministry in Geneva. The city council still had the four syndics who held the highest leadership post. They were elected annually and formed the group called the Small Council, with twenty-five members, which met at least three times a week. (When Reformation scholars refer to Geneva's city council, most of the time we are referring to the Small Council.) Next to the Small Council, Geneva had a council of two hundred people that they called the Large Council, or the Grand Council, also called the Council of Two Hundred. Within the Council of Two Hundred, there was the Council of Sixty, which met less frequently, and mostly took care of cases that involved relationships with people and institutions outside of Geneva. The members of the Council of Sixty were also members of the Council of Two Hundred.

---

[9] For the 1541 church order, or Ecclesiastical Ordinances, in English, as well as other documents published by the church in Geneva during Calvin's time, see Philip E. Hughes, ed., *Register of the Company of Pastors of Geneva at the Time of Calvin* (Grand Rapids, MI: Eerdmans, 1966). The church order was later revised in 1547, and further modifications were made in 1561.

FUN FACT

The Ecclesiastical Ordinances of 1541 were officially declared by the syndics, the Grand Council, and the Small Council of the city of Geneva, making it a city council document, even though it is a document regarding the church. By not having his name on the document, Calvin showed that the rules imposed on the people of Geneva were not just his.

The people living in Geneva might be categorized into several groups. The citizens (*citoyens*) were people born in Geneva from parents who were also citizens. The second group was the bourgeois, people not born in the city but longtime residents who had paid for the right to live there. At times there were also people who received the rights to be bourgeois without paying because they had done a service to the city. The city of Geneva gave Calvin the rights of a bourgeois at no cost on December 25, 1559, many years after he returned to the city. The bourgeois did not have the right to be elected to serve on the Small Council, but their children did. The third group was the habitants, people who were born outside of Geneva but were accepted to live, work, and rent homes in the city, but they were not electable to serve. The last group of people living in Geneva were the natifs. They were the residents coming from families who never received civic status. Some of them were from poorer areas outside of Geneva who did not have enough money to pay for their naturalization in the city.

As he reestablished his life in Geneva, Calvin underwent challenging times in his life as a family man. Idelette was in poor health most of their married life, but she managed to give birth to a baby boy, Calvin's first and only son, on July 28, 1542. They named the boy Jacques. Born prematurely, the boy died less than a month later. Idelette died a few years later, on March 29, 1549. Understandably,

Calvin was heartbroken by the deaths of his son and wife. Upon her death, Calvin wrote to Viret, expressing his loss and deep appreciation for her support of his work as a minister in the church. Calvin had promised Idelette that he would take care of her two children from her former marriage, and he kept that promise.

The Ecclesiastical Ordinances of 1541 included the regulation of church discipline and the excommunication of people who did not repent from their sins. While people were being disciplined, they were not allowed to partake in the Lord's Supper. The church order did not clearly state, however, whether the power of excommunication was in the hand of the church leaders or the civil authorities. In March of 1543 the Council of Sixty discussed this very question. It was decided that, even though church leaders had the rights to declare a person to be disciplined, the actual punishment of excommunication had to be done by the city council. Calvin did not like this decision. He requested a special meeting with the council, explaining that the rights to excommunication should rest on the authority of the Consistory, the body of church leaders, because excommunication is a churchly matter. The council finally agreed with Calvin.

Calvin's days in Geneva were mostly occupied by preaching and doing the work of a pastor to lead his congregation. On Sundays, he preached twice on particular passages from the New Testament. During the week he preached three times on the Old Testament. On Thursdays, he met with the Consistory, and on Fridays he led Bible studies for the Company of Pastors. These Friday Bible studies were called *Congrégation*. In between his preaching duties, he wrote his biblical commentaries and theological works, including the continuous work of enlarging and expanding the *Institutes*. Even when he resided in Geneva, his heart and mind were still set on the people of his home country, France, especially on the issue of Nicodemism. Calvin wrote to encourage the Huguenots to seek ways to worship the Lord openly and truthfully. If it was not possible, emigration would be the best option. But if they could not emigrate, they should refrain as far as possible from attending Catholic Mass. If their circumstances did not allow them to worship in a manner consistent with their Protestant faith, they should confess their guilt before the Lord and pray that he would deliver them from the difficult situation. As a pastor, Calvin also took care of the spiritual needs of his congregation. Geneva became a city of refuge for many people from all over Europe who faced religious persecution. Beza reported that many people from Italy, England, Spain, and other regions came to Geneva to find religious sanctuary and to join the Reformed church there.

Figure 2.1. The plaque on the spot where Calvin lived in Geneva. The writing on the plaque translates, "John Calvin lived here from 1543 to 1564, the year of his death. The house he lived in was demolished in 1706 and replaced by the current building."

Controversies. During his long ministry in Geneva, Calvin faced several controversies. Some particular polemics concerned the Anabaptists and another group called the Libertines. The Anabaptists in Geneva continued to refuse to conform themselves to the church order of Geneva. For example, they refused to abide with the rules set in the Ecclesiastical Ordinances. The Libertines, on the other hand, held to a strange way of interpreting Scripture and kept seeking new revelations. One sticking point between the Libertines and Calvin was the way they interpreted the word *spirit*. The Libertines believed that the one spirit of God lived in all people, directing everything that an individual person does, thinks, wills, and acts. In their interpretation, they blurred the distinction between good and evil, and they taught that the devil and sin were just human fantasies, not realities. They rejected the significance of Jesus as the only Savior for all of humanity. Jesus was only considered to be a good example of how people should change their attitudes from within their hearts. Calvin disagreed with all these Libertine views and wrote a tract against them.

Another matter of controversy concerned Sebastian Castellio, the Latin teacher at the Collège de Rive. In 1543, he expressed his eagerness to be ordained as a pastor. But there was a problem regarding his biblical interpretation of the Song of Songs, which Castillo viewed as the love songs of Solomon. He also disagreed with Calvin on the credal statement regarding Christ's descent into hell; for Calvin, this pointed to Christ's agony on the cross in his redemptive work for humanity. The ministers were willing to grant difference in the finer points of the interpretation of the creed, but they wanted Castellio to agree at least with the summary of the creed written in the catechism, so that when he preached, he wouldn't confuse the congregation. Castellio did not want to accept what the ministers offered. He left Geneva hoping to find work in Lausanne but later returned to Geneva. He came one Friday to the

Bible study of the Company of Pastors, interrupted the discussion, and created a scene in front of many people. Calvin did not openly fight with Castellio at that event, but later he asked the city council to ban him from the city. Castellio eventually went to Basel and taught Greek at the University of Basel.

Such events created difficulties for Calvin, but undoubtedly the most controversial event of Calvin's ministry was the execution of Michael Servetus, who was mentioned briefly before. Servetus had challenged Calvin on some key doctrinal views, including the meanings of covenant, the kingdom of God, and Jesus as the Son of God. Calvin answered Servetus's questions in writing under his pseudonym Charles d'Espeville. Not satisfied with what Calvin wrote, Servetus continued the debate. He published a book titled *Christianismi restitutio*, or *Restoration of Christianity*, in which he rejected many of the standard orthodox beliefs of the church, including the doctrine of the Trinity. He published the book anonymously with only the initials M. S. V. as the author. The initials M and V stood for Michael Villanovanus, the name taken after his hometown in Spain, the town of Villaneuve. The book was printed in Vienne, a town not far from Lyon, in January 1553. In the book, Servetus attacked Calvin personally, saying that Calvin's doctrine was wrong and that the correct doctrine—the one he promoted— had been silenced by both the Roman Catholic and Protestant churches. In February 1553, Servetus was imprisoned by Catholic officials because of his heretical views, and he was examined by the Inquisition. He was, however, able to escape the prison in Vienne. The Inquisition declared him a heretic in his absence, and because of his views, the scandal that he created, and his escape from prison, his capital punishment was carried out in effigy: a picture of him was burned. In the eyes of the Church of Rome, Servetus was already a condemned person in Vienne. For some reason, however, on August 13, 1553, he traveled to Geneva and appeared in the audience when Calvin was lecturing.

Servetus was arrested in Geneva with thirty-nine points of official complaints. Servetus's trial started on August 17, 1553. The trial included a long discussion on the problems that Servetus had caused not just in Vienne but also in Basel and Strasbourg. The magistrate of Geneva sent a letter to Vienne to ask for explanations on the circumstances of Servetus's arrest and how he was able to escape. Vienne refused to reply but required that Servetus be extradited. Geneva refused and proceeded with its own trial. Servetus had to respond in writing to points that Calvin and other ministers in Geneva considered heretical. The Genevan council sought counsel from other cities including Zurich, Bern, Basel, and Schaffhausen on how to deal with Servetus. All of them declared Servetus's teaching to be false, but they also left it up to Geneva to determine the punishment. Finally, the city council decided on October 26, 1553, that Servetus would be burned at the stake. Calvin tried to change the punishment into a less severe one by arguing for beheading because he thought that mode of execution quicker and less painful, but the city council rejected Calvin's request. Servetus was executed the following day.

Before Servetus's execution, Calvin and Farel visited Servetus in his prison cell. Servetus asked for mercy and a change in the punishment. Calvin stated that the punishment had nothing to do with Servetus's personal attack against him. Both men asked him to change his view on the doctrine of the Trinity, but he refused. Before Servetus was burned at the stake, one of the syndics read the charges against him that included heretical views against the Trinity, infant baptism, and many other items. Just before he died, Servetus cried out, "Jesus, Son of the eternal God, take pity on me."[10]

---

[10]An English translation of the full record of Servetus's trial is published in Hughes, *Register of the Company of Pastors*, 223-83.

Later critics of Calvin often lack a full historical perspective when criticizing his connection to the execution of Michael Servetus. When approaching this difficult event, it is important to understand that Servetus would have been condemned as a heretic wherever he was, not just in Geneva. It is also important to note that the decision to burn him at the stake was not made by Calvin but by the city council. Calvin was not in charge in the execution, but that has not prevented people from unfairly placing the blame for Servetus's death at Calvin's feet.

Another theological controversy that Calvin faced earlier in his career concerned Jerome Bolsec on the doctrine of predestination. Bolsec had formerly been a monk in Paris, but he became a Protestant after running away from the city. Bolsec challenged Calvin's view of free will at a pastors' Bible study meeting, or the *Congrégation*, on May 15, 1551. According to Beza, when Bolsec first debated the doctrine, Calvin wasn't in the room. But when Calvin arrived, the debate escalated. Because of the chaos he caused at that meeting, Bolsec was arrested. His trial was a heated one, with some people defending him and his doctrine. The ministers of Geneva consulted with others from Bern, Basel, and Zurich to ask for their opinions on the doctrine. All the ministers from the three cities rejected the teaching that Bolsec upheld. On December 18, 1551, Calvin made a long presentation on the doctrine of election, arguing that God elects each individual for salvation, contradicting Bolsec's view of universal salvation. The city council accepted Calvin's doctrine, and on December 21, 1551, Geneva permanently banned Bolsec from the city. The controversy surrounding Bolsec and other events reveal the complicated dynamic between civil and ecclesiastical authorities in Geneva. Calvin is sometimes inaccurately regarded as having established a theocracy in Geneva, when in fact the civil leaders maintained and exercised their own authority.

Sometimes, seemingly small events led to larger controversies. For example, a Genevan man by the name of Philibert Berthelier was excommunicated because of drunkenness. On September 1, 1553, about one-and-a-half years after the initial excommunication, he requested that the Consistory allow him to partake in the Lord's Supper again. Even though it had been agreed that it was the Consistory who had the authority to excommunicate and to reinstate a person, the city council decided that Berthelier was allowed to partake in the sacrament again. Calvin protested to the city council, but his protest was ignored. On September 3, during a service of the Lord's Supper, Calvin preached, and he made it clear that he disliked the decision of the city council. Berthelier, however, did not partake in the Lord's Supper that morning. Nonetheless, viewing the council's handling of the matter as a profound betrayal, Calvin's evening sermon sounded like it would be the last he would ever preach in Geneva.

On September 7, 1553, the ministers protested to the city council. The members of the council asked for a clear explanation on how the 1541 church ordinances should be interpreted. Calvin explained that it was the Consistory, not the city council, that had the authority to excommunicate and to reinstate people to the Lord's Supper. The council decided on September 18 that, from that point on, they would stand with Calvin's explanation of the church order. But this decision did not last for long. In early November, Berthelier asked again if he could be allowed to partake in the Lord's Supper. The Consistory rejected the request. But on November 7, the city council stated that the Consistory should not decide to reject requests without consulting the council. It nullified the decision of the Consistory and allowed Berthelier to take the sacrament. Calvin rejected the council's decision. Because of this situation, the council asked the opinions of the churches in Bern, Zurich, Basel, and Schaffhausen. These four churches gave different responses that satisfied neither the ministers nor the city council. After a long while, on October 24, 1554, the council appointed a committee to look into the matter. On January 24, 1555, the committee decided that the Council of Sixty and the Council of Two Hundred should agree to accept the regulation of the 1541 Ecclesiastical Ordinances. Everybody agreed that the authority to excommunicate should be in the hands of the Consistory. The matter finally came to a rest with that decision.

Throughout his ministry, Calvin's desire was to create a place where people could truly worship God and live faithful Christian lives. Inevitably, though, this led to conflicts. Pierre Ameaux was a member of the Small Council and made a living playing cards. Following a series of unfortunate events, he divorced his wife. He wanted to remarry, and finally he received permission. But Ameaux made a bitter accusation against Calvin, suggesting that he was the cause of his divorce. In addition, he called Calvin a derogatory name based on Calvin's French origin. Ameaux was arrested for slander. Because the Small Council could not decide between a mild or a more severe punishment for Ameaux, it asked for the Council of Two Hundred to decide. The latter decided on a mild punishment, in which Ameaux had to kneel before Calvin to ask for forgiveness. Calvin also agreed with the mild punishment. He visited Ameaux in prison to talk with him before the punishment was to be carried out. However, later Ameaux caused a more serious issue. He spread rumors that Calvin was a heretic and that the church wasn't doing anything to stop Calvin's heresy. This time, Calvin wanted a more severe punishment for Ameaux. The punishment was changed into one in which he had to wear penitence garb, have his head shaved, and carry a burning torch to walk from the prison to the city hall. When he arrived there, he had to kneel between the two doors, ask God for forgiveness, and beg the city council for mercy.

Another controversy centered on the prohibition on dancing. This prohibition was already in place before Calvin arrived in Geneva. Ami Perrin, the head of the artillery, violated the regulation. Perrin's wife made matters worse by coming before the Consistory and angrily charging the members of the Consistory, who had previously charged her father with adultery, as having a grudge against her family. Calvin wanted to talk with Perrin after a church service one Sunday, but the latter did not go to church that Sunday. Calvin wrote a letter explaining the position of the church, but Perrin did not want to accept the explanation. The problem between Calvin and Perrin persisted. In August 1546, Perrin's brother-in-law got married. When the minister asked him whether he would accept the bride as his wife, he did not hear the question. Instead of saying yes, he shook his head. Upon seeing the comical situation, Perrin laughed. The council looked at this as an irreverent act, and Perrin received punishment from the council. It also happened that the day before the wedding, Perrin's mother had beaten up a family member in a fight. This was an unacceptable act in the eyes of the Consistory. She was summoned before the Consistory, but she ran away. Calvin had to navigate difficult courses just to deal with this one family. Later, Ami Perrin protested the city council regarding the imprisonment of his wife, who was charged with excessive dancing. Because of his conduct, he was arrested and then stripped of his position as the head of the artillery. At the trial, he was also charged with having served in the coronation of Henry II in Paris, but the charge did not have strong evidence. Eventually, Perrin was released from prison, and in 1549, he was elected a syndic, which only further complicated matters for Calvin.

The frictions with Perrin only ended in 1555 when he and his supporters were soundly defeated in a dispute about the French refugees in Geneva. There were about 120 refugees coming to Geneva, and they received the right to live in the city. Some of the established Genevan citizens, including Perrin's family, did not like the refugees and tried to limit their rights. They made a proposal to forbid the refugees to vote or to carry arms for ten years, even though they had earned their civic rights in Geneva. On May 6, 1555, the city council rejected the proposal. On May 16, more than five hundred people protested against the city council. After the protest was over, many of the protesters were invited to a meal sponsored by the leaders of the group that supported Perrin's family, called *enfants de Geneve*, or the children of Geneva. Unrest ensued on the streets of Geneva. Another syndic by the name of Henri Aubert tried to maintain order by arresting one of the people causing the riot. Perrin snatched away Aubert's staff of office. The city council launched an investigation, and the ringleaders of the riot were arrested. The Small and Great Councils looked into the matter, but Perrin had fled the city by then. Twelve people who led the riot were condemned. Three were executed and nine were exiled from Geneva. From that time on, Calvin received more support from the people and leaders of Geneva, and he was able to focus his work on further reforming the church.

The reformation of education. Not everything in Calvin's ministry was characterized by controversy. When he returned to Geneva in 1541, Calvin planned to start an academy in Geneva. The various struggles he faced prevented him from executing the plan right away. Only when the situation in Geneva finally became calmer and the people accepted him warmly was he able to work toward establishing the academy. On his way to Frankfurt in 1556, he made a stop in Strasbourg to talk with Jean Sturm, the head of the city's academy, who provided insight into starting an academy. In 1558, Calvin identified a good location to build the academy, a piece of land not far from Bourg-de-Four hospital. The academy was founded the next year.

The curriculum of the academy in Geneva was divided into two parts: the *schola privata* and the *schola publica*. In the *schola privata* the students first learned to read and write in both Latin and French.[11] After mastering those subjects, they moved up to studying Latin and Greek thinkers. School was not in session on Wednesdays. On Saturdays the students reviewed the lessons of the week and studied the catechism for the following Sunday. Each day would start with a prayer and psalm singing. In addition, the students recited the Lord's Prayer, the Apostles' Creed, and the Ten Commandments. Once the students finished with the *schola privata*, they could move up to the *schola publica*. At this level, the students had to sign the confession of faith and take twenty-seven courses from specific teachers. For example, the Hebrew teacher taught Old Testament exegesis, the Greek teacher instructed the students in reading the works of Greek philosophers and poets, and the teachers who specialized in the arts taught mathematics, sciences, and rhetoric. Students who focused on rhetoric prepared themselves to be ministers or lawyers. Calvin's emphasis on education, seen in the founding of the academy, is one of his lasting legacies and influences on the Reformed church.

That tradition was carried on by Theodore Beza, who had been a widely respected Greek teacher in Lausanne since 1549. Beza came to Geneva in 1558 and was installed as a Greek teacher in November of that year. On June 5, 1559, Beza was installed as the rector of the academy and delivered an opening address at the church of St. Pierre in Geneva. Afterward, the secretary of the city read the statutes of the academy, and all the teachers took an oath and subscribed to the confession of faith of the church of Geneva. Later, Beza would become Calvin's successor in Geneva.

---

[11]For a detailed study of the Genevan academy, see Karin Maag, *Seminary or University: The Genevan Academy and Reformed Higher Education, 1560–1620* (Brookfield, CT: Ashgate, 1995).

A remarkable life, an unmarked grave. Calvin was not always in good physical health. He suffered several illnesses early on, and a more precipitous decline began in 1556, a year after he gained the victory against the Perrinists that sealed his place in Geneva. Beza reported that on May 10 of that year, Calvin had a bad fever. He still managed to preach, but while preaching, his illness became so bad that he had to leave the pulpit. There was a rumor in Noyon, fanned by the Roman Catholics, that he had already died. He recovered, but his health got worse from that point on. He often suffered from fevers and migraines. At one point, his illness lasted off and on for eight months, causing him to be so weak that he needed another person to assist him to walk up to the pulpit.

Calvin continued to suffer from a variety of painful ailments, including kidney stones, gout, gallstones, stomach pains, and asthma. On February 2, 1564, he delivered his last lecture on the Old Testament, and he preached his last sermon at church on February 6. On March 31, he met for the last time with the ministers. He attended a church service for the last time on Easter Sunday, April 2 of that year, where he partook in the Lord's Supper.

On April 25, 1564, Calvin asked for Pierre Chenelat, a notary in Geneva, and he dictated his last will to him. Praising God, Calvin expressed his gratitude for the grace that God had given him. In the will, he stated that when he died, he wanted to be buried in an unmarked grave, without much ceremonial pomp. What was important for him was the final resurrection that Jesus has promised to all his people. He bequeathed his few personal belongings to his brother Antoine, the daughter of his half sister, and his brother's children. On April 27, Calvin wanted to say goodbye to the syndics and members of the Small Council, so they visited him at home. He thanked them for their support of his work and for being his friends. The next day, he said his farewell to the ministers of the church. His old friend Farel, though already very advanced in age, made the effort to visit him in Geneva. He was delighted to receive Farel in his home, and he managed to see some friends visiting him at home for a few more days until, on May 27, 1564, Calvin took his last breath. He died peacefully. Following his wish, he was buried in the common cemetery of Plein Palais without any gravestone.

In 2009, as a part of the commemoration of the five-hundredth anniversary of Calvin's birth, I had the opportunity to visit Geneva, the city where Calvin did most of his work in reforming the church. In addition to academic conferences that honored the life and works of Calvin, I attended worship at St. Pierre, the church where Calvin mainly preached, and visited the *auditoir*, where he lectured and conducted Bible study week in and week out. I also had the opportunity to attend La Madeleine, the other church in Geneva where church services were conducted. But the deepest impression I brought home from my visit to Geneva was the plainness of the cemetery where Calvin is believed to be buried. Nobody today can tell with certainty where his grave is. While I wish, on the one hand, that we knew where he is buried, on the other hand, I am glad that Calvin's intention has been fulfilled: those who want to commemorate his life can focus their attention less on his remarkable achievements and more on the remarkable grace and promises of God.

Suggestions for Further Reading

Bouwsma, William, *John Calvin: A Sixteenth-Century Portrait*. New York: Oxford University Press, 1989.

Brewer, Brian, and David Whitford. *Calvin and the Early Reformation*. Boston: Brill, 2019.

Cottret, Bernard. *Calvin: A Biography*. Grand Rapids, MI: Eerdmans, 2000.

Gordon, Bruce. *John Calvin's Institutes of the Christian Religion: A Biography*. Princeton, NJ: Princeton University Press, 2016.

Parker, T. H. L. *John Calvin: A Biography*. Louisville, KY: Westminster John Knox, 2007.

Selderhuis, Herman. *John Calvin: A Pilgrim's Life*. Downers Grove, IL: IVP Academic, 2009.

Van Den Berg, Machiel. *Friends of Calvin*. Translated by Reinder Bruinsma. Grand Rapids, MI: Eerdmans, 2009.

3

Frequently Asked Questions About Calvin

As an influential theologian and pastor in the history of the church, Calvin has been the center of many people's attention for almost five hundred years. Undoubtedly, he was a complex individual who lived within his own cultural context and who faced, like all pastors, challenges in his church work. The thoughts and legacy he left behind are enormous, and many Protestant churches today still apply his thoughts, teachings, and practices, whether they realize it or not. At the same time, many people today look at him and his thoughts with intense dislike. All of this leaves us with questions that need to be answered or presuppositions that need to be rethought. In what follows, I will attempt to answer some of the most frequently asked questions about Calvin and his legacy.

Did Calvin Invent the Doctrine of Predestination?

More than a few people mistakenly believe that Calvin was the originator of the doctrine of predestination. This notion likely stems from the emphasis placed on it within Calvinist circles and the differences between Calvinism and Arminianism. Calvinism comes out of the theology of Calvin, which, based on passages such

as Romans 8:2-30 and Ephesians 1:1-14, affirms that God has pre-
destinated certain people to receive eternal salvation based solely
on God's decision in eternity, while others are eternally condemned,
a doctrine sometimes called "double predestination." According to
this view, humans can do nothing to earn God's gift of salvation.
Salvation is based solely on God's decision. On the other hand, the
Arminian position, the view attributed to Jacob Arminius (1560–
1609), a Dutch theologian who at one time studied at the Genevan
academy under Theodore Beza, states that humans have a say in
matters concerning their salvation. According to his view, God predestines people based on God's foreknowledge of whether people
will accept the gospel. In other words, in eternity, God chooses or
rejects people for salvation based on their foreseen faith. The Calvinist position declared at the Synod of Dordt rejects this view. It
states that God elects people for salvation for the purpose of faith,
or that the elect will have faith. Therefore, faith is not the prereq-
uisite for election. Importantly, both Calvinist and Arminian views
affirm that God predestines people; the basis of that decision is the
difference between them.

Long before this dispute, however, Christians had affirmed the
doctrine of predestination. One notable example was Augustine
(354–430), who, following the apostle Paul, taught that salvation
depends entirely on God's choosing of us in Christ before the foundation of the world (Eph 1:4). God's choice of us is not because we
are already holy, but in order that we might become holy. Based on
God's choosing of us, according to Augustine, we are adopted to be
the children of God. In this way, Augustine shows that we do not
have any part in gaining our salvation. Rather, we receive it only
because of God's grace.[1] In the sixteenth century, Calvin reiterated

---

[1] Augustine, "A Treatise on the Predestination of the Saints," 37, in *Nicene and Post-
Nicene Fathers*, Series 1, ed. Philip Schaff (1886–1889; repr. Grand Rapids, MI: Eerdmans, 1997), 5:516.

what Augustine wrote long before. He, too, believed that salvation is due only to God's grace.

Did Calvin Invent the Acronym TULIP?

Another commonly held view about Calvin is that he was directly responsible for the creation of the acronym TULIP, which people use as a mnemonic device to simplify the five points of the doctrine of salvation within Reformed theology. The T in the acronym stands for "total depravity," the U for "unconditional election," the L for "limited atonement," the I for "irresistible grace," and the P for the "perseverance of the saints."

Calvin did not start the use of the acronym. In fact, Calvin did not even formulate the five points of Calvinism that many people use to summarize the doctrine of salvation within the Reformed tradition. The five points came into being in the early seventeenth century, about fifty years after Calvin died. When Theodore Beza was leading the church in Geneva, another region in Europe, the Netherlands underwent big changes. For quite some time the region called the Low Countries—modern-day Belgium, French Flanders, and the Netherlands—was under the power of King Philip II of Spain, a predominantly Roman Catholic country. In the 1580s, the Netherlands was able to break free from Spain. The break with Spain also gave rise to the Dutch Republic establishing itself as independent in determining its own religious identity. Partly as a reaction against Roman Catholic Spain, it adopted Reformed theology and church practices as its religious identity. Within this context, Arminius came to Geneva to study under Beza in order to become a minister. But while in Geneva, Arminius found that he disagreed with the Reformed view of double predestination, the belief that God elected some people for eternal salvation and some for damnation.

Arminius left Geneva quietly to continue his study in Basel. He returned to the Netherlands to minister at a church in Amsterdam in 1587 and later became a professor of theology at Leiden. While a pastor in Amsterdam, he voiced his disagreements with the Reformed view of supralapsarianism that Beza and other ministers in Geneva firmly held. His 1606 address in front of the university, titled "On Reconciling Religious Dissensions Among Christians," created a great stir by challenging the basic tenets of Reformed beliefs. He also suggested a revision to the Belgic Confession and the Heidelberg Catechism, two of the most important confessional standards within churches that had adopted the teachings of Calvin. Arminius was opposed by Franciscus Gomarus, a staunch follower of Beza and supporter of the Reformed church in Geneva. The debates over predestination and supralapsarianism continued even after Arminius's death in 1609. His followers, known as the Remonstrants, meaning "those who opposed," continued expanding his teachings. Theological arguments continued between the followers of Calvin and Beza's views and the Remonstrants.

Supralapsarianism is a view held by Reformed theologians that logically (as opposed to temporally), God's decree to elect people for salvation precedes God's decree to create and to permit humanity's fall into sin. The word *supra* means "above," and *lapsus* means "fall." The opposite of this position is *infralapsarianism* (*infra* means "below"), which holds that God's decree to elect people for salvation follows his decree to create and to allow humanity's fall.

In 1610, the Remonstrants wrote up a document that summarized their view of the doctrine of salvation. They outlined their direct opposition to the view of double predestination, which they refuted by reformulating it with five main points. The first point of the Articles of Remonstrance says that, in matters of salvation, God chooses to save those who will believe in Christ and punishes those who will not believe in Christ. The second main point says that Christ died for all people, but only those who believe in him will be saved. The third point states that all people in the world are sinners and are therefore unable to save themselves; they are only saved by Christ and in Christ. The fourth point declares that God pours out his grace of salvation, and people can reject God's grace; those who reject grace will not be saved. The last point says that, while God keeps believers in his hands, they are capable, because of their own negligence, to return to evil and thereby lose their salvation.

The Netherlands in the earliest decade of the seventeenth century also saw a sharp competition between two political groups, one led by Prince Maurice of Nassau and the other by Johan van Oldenbarnevelt. Prince Maurice agreed with the teachings of Calvin and the church of Geneva. The Remonstrants, meanwhile, found support from Oldenbarnevelt. By then, the Reformed (or Calvinistic) beliefs were already the positions held by the Dutch government. And so this theological dispute became intermingled with political struggles. These problems escalated until 1618, when the Dutch States-General called for a national synod in the city of Dordrecht. The States-General invited Reformed delegates from other countries and regions of Europe to attend the meetings, which were held from November 13, 1618, to May 9, 1619. The synod is famously called the Synod of Dordt, using the shortened version of the city's name. The results of the synod are called the Canons of Dordt, in which the five articles of the Remonstrants are repudiated one article at a time. The first point says that God chooses people to salvation by his decision and not because of anything that people do. The second point says that Jesus' death and resurrection did not just open the door for people to be saved but actually saved those whom

God has chosen. Dordt responded to the Remonstrants' third and fourth points together, stating that all people are born sinners and cannot save themselves. People can only be saved by God's grace, which powerfully transforms them. And finally, the last point declares that God keeps those he has saved firmly in his hands, and therefore our salvation is secure. So, technically, Dordt responded in four points, with the third point consisting of two parts.

But the acronym TULIP was not used even by the Synod of Dordt. As far as we can tell, the acronym started to be used in the early twentieth century in America. When theologians and church leaders tried to help others remember the five points, they used the acronym. TULIP may be attributable to a minister by the name of Cleland Boyd McAfee, who taught at McCormick Theological Seminary in Chicago and later moved to Brooklyn, New York. A man by the name of William H. Vail reported hearing a speech by Dr. McAfee in 1905 in which the latter cleverly used of the acronym TULIP to summarize the five points of Calvinism.[2]

If you take a close look at the acronym, you can see that the ordering of the points does not follow the same order of the points raised by the Remonstrants and therefore did not follow the points made in the Canons of Dordt. Instead, it begins with the total depravity of all people (the T in the acronym), then affirms the unconditional nature of God's choosing of people to salvation (the U in the acronym), the limitedness of Christ's saving work on the cross only to people God chooses to salvation (the L in the acronym), the fact that God's grace cannot be rejected and therefore is irresistible

---

[2]William H. Vail, "The Five Points of Calvinism Historically Considered," *The Outlook*, June 21, 1913, compiled as vol. 104 (May–August 1913): 394-95. For further discussion on this topic, see Kenneth J. Stewart, "The Points of Calvinism: Retrospect and Prospect," *Scottish Bulletin of Evangelical Theology* 26, no. 2 (2008): 187-203; and his very helpful book, *Ten Myths About Calvinism: Recovering the Breadth of Reformed Tradition* (Downers Grove, IL: IVP Academic, 2011), 75-96. In that book, see especially "Appendix: The Earliest Known Reference to the TULIP Acronym" (291–92), which includes a reproduction of the 1913 article from *The Outlook*.

(the I in the acronym), and finally the belief that God's people will persevere to the end (the P in the acronym). Personally, I find the creation of the acronym too forced, not to mention historically and textually inaccurate. My guess is that the acronym TULIP developed in part because the conflict between the Calvinists and the Remonstrants happened in the Netherlands, and the tulip is the national flower of the Netherlands. Of course, if we want to be historically accurate and follow the order of the original articles and canons, the acronym should be U-L-T-I-P.

At any rate, the acronym did not originate with Calvin, and it would be a mischaracterization for us to identify it with him. While the five points of the Synod of Dordt are based on what Calvin taught, they are not the same as what Calvin wrote. I find that Christians who only look at Calvin as somehow closely tied to the acronym miss the depth and beauty of Calvin's life, teachings, and influence in the history of the church. There is much more to Calvin than just a later formulation of the doctrine of salvation (or soteriology) as expressed in the five points.

Is There a Difference Between Calvinism and Reformed Theology?

You may have noticed my use of the terms such as *Calvinism* and *Calvinists*; *Reformed* and *Reformed theology*; *Arminianism*; and *Remonstrants*. The term *Calvinism* refers to the theological system or belief that finds its roots generally in the teaching of Calvin. By now, I am sure you can deduce that there may be a slight difference between Calvin's own theological beliefs and those expanded by his followers, which are known as Calvinism. The word *Calvinist* refers to people who embrace and largely agree with the teaching of Calvinism. As Richard Muller has explained, in the sixteenth century, the terms *Calvinism* and *Calvinist* were used by people who disagreed with Calvin—most of them were Lutherans—and who opposed his view of the Lord's Supper. So, originally, the use of these terms reflected a split among the Reformers who had separated themselves from Rome. The terms *Reformed* and *Reformed theology* are related to the belief system and the theology of the group of sixteenth-century Reformers in which Calvin had a significant part. The adjective *Reformed* is usually used to show the characteristic of churches or people who embrace a confessional tradition that was started in the middle of the sixteenth century as formulated in confessional documents such as the Belgic and Gallican Confessions, the Heidelberg Catechism, and the Thirty-nine Articles. These documents found their core teachings in Calvin's theology and were originated by groups of churches outside of Geneva. Therefore, you can see that there was a continuity between Calvin and later Reformed believers. The cause of this continuity is not the individuality of Calvin's theology, but the universality of the theological view itself.[3] Generally speaking, the adjective is largely synonymous with *Calvinist*, but there are some differences; the Reformed tradition is broader and more expansive than just Calvin's theology, though it is clearly indebted to it.

Similar to Calvinism, *Arminianism* is the belief system that largely follows the main teaching of one person, in this case, Arminius. Just as there are differences between the teachings of Calvin and those of Calvinism, there are variations between Arminius and later Arminianism, as seen with the Remonstrants, but they share common emphases on the role of God's foreknowledge of human decisions in salvation and the human exercise of free will.

---

[3]For further understanding of these distinctions, see Richard Muller, "Was Calvin a Calvinist?," in *Calvin and the Reformed Tradition: On the Work of Christ and the Order of Salvation* (Grand Rapids, MI: Baker Academic, 2012), 51–69. See also his two-part journal article, "Calvin and the 'Calvinists': Assessing Continuities and Discontinuities Between the Reformers and Orthodoxy," *Calvin Theological Journal* 30 (1995): 345-75; 31 (1996): 125-60.

Was Calvin an Angry Person, or Was There Another Side to Him?

Several people today have the impression that Calvin was a dour, angry, stern, and humorless person. Many factors contribute to this impression: his strong defense of the truth of the Word of God against its adversaries, which sometimes led to disputes with others; his tireless effort to reform the Genevans' moral life by way of the Consistory; and the smear campaigns that his opponents waged against him. Despite people's negative impression of him, Calvin had another side that showed tenderness of heart and deep care for people. Unfortunately, this side is often hidden because it is overshadowed by the tougher, strong personality and theological opinions that he demonstrated.

Calvin wholeheartedly sought to defend the true teaching of the church based on his careful interpretation of the Bible. In his time, he had seen the misinterpretation of the Bible and abusive behaviors of the clergy of the Church of Rome that grew out of medieval practices. He wrote vehemently against them. In addition, as he progressed in his work of reforming the church, he faced oppositions from his contemporaries on certain theological views. As the era of the Reformation continued, differing biblical interpretations also came to the surface. Calvin faced certain groups within the evangelical camp in his days. The Anabaptists, with their rejection of infant baptism and separation from society, were front and center in directly opposing Calvin's stance. In addition, his differing theological interpretation on the Lord's Supper against the Lutherans and the Church of Rome pitched him at odds with these two theological streams. On top of this, theological debates on predestination, among other issues, engendered his engagement in polemics against some opponents.

Calvin never hesitated to use strong words when he had disagreements with his opponents. When he thought that his opponents did not demonstrate sound reasoning abilities or stood against the Word of God, he might call them a dog or a swine, which were regarded as unworthy animals. He also used other disparaging expressions to characterize his opponents. For instance, he wrote that Servetus, who rejected the orthodox view of the Trinity, held to "brutish ravings," and he called Valentine Gentile, another trinitarian heretic, a monster.[4] This way of writing was a rhetorical style that he used to make his point to his readers. The same technique was used by many others of his day. But it's understandable why such harsh words contributed to the impression that Calvin was an angry person.

Another factor in creating this impression was Calvin's strong insistence that the Genevans must lead their lives as true Christians, which was the impetus for his demand for a Consistory. This body called before it people who had been found committing sins, demonstrating unacceptable behavior, skipping church, or performing many other offenses. While the intention of the Consistory was good, it understandably became a terrifying entity for those summoned to appear. Moreover, even though the syndic was technically the one leading the questioning, Calvin often asked the most questions. He sincerely wanted the people to live as true children of God, and he saw that right Christian beliefs must be followed by right conduct in daily practice. In Calvin's view, the Consistory was the way to do this, and he did not hesitate to take that route, even when the result was people's misperception of him as a stern or harsh leader.

A third factor in this impression of Calvin was the smear campaigns by his opponents, which have persisted even to this day. For example, Jerome Bolsec held a grudge against Calvin that started with their differing opinions on the doctrine of predestination.

---

[4]John Calvin, *Institutes of the Christian Religion* [1559], ed. John T. McNeill, trans. Ford Lewis Battles (Philadelphia: Westminster, 1960). I.13.22-23.

After Bolsec was banned from the city, he continued expressing his disagreement with Calvin, even calling the Reformer a heretic and an antichrist. The execution of Servetus in 1553 gave Bolsec an even greater opportunity, through tracts that he published, to label Calvin a tyrant. In 1577, more than a decade after Calvin had died, Bolsec published a biography of Calvin, *Vie de Calvin*. In almost every way, it was a direct opposite of Beza's biography of the Reformer. In his book, Bolsec wrote a scathing story about Calvin as a young man in Noyon being charged with sodomy and as a punishment being branded with a mark of the fleur-de-lis. This false accusation against Calvin might have been based on Bolsec's careless use or misappropriation of a record from Noyon about a certain Jean Cauvin, a vicar of Noyon, who in 1553 received punishment for a reckless lifestyle. But looking at the date of this record, it's obvious it wasn't the Reformer, who by that time was already in Geneva. Furthermore, Bolsec's biography paints a grim picture of Calvin's last days in an effort to show that he died a cursed person. He wrote that lice and vermin covered his whole body and that he had a bad ulcer that emitted a terrible odor, and worms ate his body even while he was still alive. Besides Bolsec, other authors wrote biographies of Calvin that portrayed him as a heretic and an insufferable tyrant. According to these biographies, published by Catholic authors after Calvin's death, he led Geneva as a cruel dictator. They were later translated into several languages and saw wide distribution well into the seventeenth century. As is the case with most negative publicity, these pictures of Calvin contributed to the impression, which people have held throughout several centuries now, that Calvin was an angry, despotic leader.

But Calvin was not the dour person some people believed him to be. He was a caring, loving pastor who stood firmly on the teaching of the Bible. The focus of his work was not just on the spiritual needs of the people but also on their day-to-day living.

He wanted the people to live as true Christians who expressed their faith through their daily lives. Furthermore, his stay in Geneva saw the city grow as a place of refuge for the poor and those facing religious persecution in other parts of Europe. The hospital in the city cared for all those in need, including foreigners. When Calvin explains the doctrine of creation in the *Institutes*, he points to the beauty of creation. By calling creation "the theater of God's glory," he invites his readers to be immersed in and enjoy God's goodness in creation, to take delight in different kinds of foods and tastes, and to give thanks for the variety of colors and smells of the flowers.[5]

Calvin acknowledged that he could be too strong and vehement when arguing. As he was about to die, the Genevan city leaders came to his house. He thanked them for their partnership in leading the city with him and also for their willingness to be patient with him. He apologized for his forcefulness, which he often carried to excess. He also said that he had asked for forgiveness from God for this shortcoming, and that he believed God had forgiven him. Then he added that, when it comes to teaching the true doctrine of the Bible, he had not and would never be shaken because he had taught with utmost sincerity and certainty.

A few days before Calvin died, the ministers of Geneva came to his house to celebrate the Lord's Supper and to fellowship with him. Pentecost was only two days away, and the church would celebrate the sacrament that Sunday. Beza wrote that, after eating, Calvin felt very weak and asked to be carried into the bedroom adjacent to the place where the ministers were gathered. Calvin spoke to the ministers with a smile on his face, saying that the wall separating the two rooms made him absent physically, but it would not prevent him from being present with them in spirit. A friendly joke such as

---

[5]Calvin, *Institutes* III.10.2.

this is deeply embedded in his theology, and it reveals a side of Calvin that not many people know.

Did Calvin Hold an Optimistic or Pessimistic View of Human Nature?

On a first read, Calvin might appear to hold a low view of human beings. In the *Institutes* he writes,

> There is indeed nothing that [hu]man's nature seeks more eagerly than to be flattered. Accordingly, when [their] nature becomes aware that its gifts are highly esteemed, it tends to be unduly credulous about them. It is thus no wonder that the majority of [people] have erred so perniciously in this respect. For, since blind self-love is innate in all mortals, they are most freely persuaded that nothing inheres in themselves that deserves to be considered hateful.

He later adds,

> He who scrutinizes and examines himself according to the standard of divine judgment finds nothing to lift his heart to self-confidence. And the more deeply he examines himself, the more dejected he becomes until, utterly deprived of all such assurance, he leaves nothing to himself with which to direct his life aright.[6]

In addition, in article four of the 1538 edition of his *Catechism*, he describes humans as "impure, profane, and abominable to God" and that human prudence, "blind and entangled in limitless errors," is always in direct opposition to God.[7] Taken as they are, these quotes seem to indicate that Calvin had a low view of human beings.

---

[6]Calvin, *Institutes* II.1.2-3.

[7]John Calvin, article 4, *Catechism* 1538, in I. John Hesselink, *Calvin's First Catechism: A Commentary* (Louisville, KY: Westminster John Knox Press, 1997), 9.

But we need to understand that he was speaking about human beings in their fallen condition.

Knowing ourselves, Calvin explains in the *Institutes,* begins with understanding that, at creation, God gives human beings his favors generously and that humans are equipped with natural excellence. This is all God's goodness toward humans. However, since Adam and Eve fell into sin, all humans have lost the original goodness that God initially gave them. The knowledge of self now prompts humans to see their need in their sinful state, bringing them to seek help from God. Thus, by showing how bad humanity's condition is because of sin, Calvin seeks to show that humans cannot help themselves to get out of their misery. Good works will never help humans escape their wretched condition. Only through the work of Jesus can humans find help and salvation. Christ is the one restoring in human beings the image of God that was originally given in creation but broken because of Adam's sin. The restoration of the image of God in humans, through the saving work of Christ, brings humans to enjoy once again the goodness of God and creation. Therefore, in light of the redemptive work of Christ, humans can fulfill what God intends them to be and do. Thus, we can say that, while Calvin has a pessimistic view of humans in their sinful state, he actually has an optimistic view of human beings in the context of redemption in Christ.

What Did Calvin Think About Economic Exchange?

Calvin saw both the dangers and the potential benefits of money. He warned people not to fall into the temptation of the love of money, because money is a part of the system of fallen humanity. Sin has tainted people's way of interacting with each other, including the economic exchanges between people. Calvin understood well that commerce was an integral part of life in Geneva. The city leaders, according to Calvin, had the duty to regulate

trade, especially to prevent greedy people from taking advantage
of the poor. He was not against the market, but he was cautious
about people using it merely for their own wealth. He proposed a
5 percent charge on legitimate loans and was instrumental in the
establishment of a public bank. He also taught clearly about the
necessity of fair wages, controlled prices for food, and good
working environments. The Consistory in Geneva summoned
people who practiced usury, price gouging, and fraud. Calvin lived
in a time when Geneva was undergoing significant changes, including economic changes. He had to balance the biblical command
to love one another with the need for people to live well and
be prosperous.

According to Calvin, people who were able to help others should
make every effort to care for the poor. Giving was not just the act of
donating money but, more importantly, people thinking of others
and seeking to eliminate suffering. In his sermons on Deuteronomy,
Calvin repeatedly called on his hearers to take action and apply the
Christian belief in giving by helping those in need. Care for the poor,
the refugees, and the sick took center stage in Geneva, with the aim
of the hospital being to care for all these people, not just the sick.
When funds for the Geneva hospital, which existed before Calvin's
time, ran low, Calvin took the initiative to collect funds, called the
bourse française (the French fund), to provide the money needed.
Calvin's way of establishing a truly Christian community in Geneva
was through church and the Consistory.

Did Calvin Write Commentaries on All the Books of the Bible?

No, Calvin did not write commentaries on all the books of the Bible.
But he wrote on *nearly* every book of the Bible. When we look at
Calvin's interpretation of the Bible, we need to distinguish between
his straightforward commentaries and his lectures on specific
books of the Bible. The commentaries were based on his studies,

which followed his strict exegetical methodology. The lectures, on the other hand, were delivered in front of students, ministers, and other interested parties. Based on the account of Nicolas Colladon, a Calvin biographer, when Calvin delivered his lectures, he mainly read from the Bible and gave explanation on the passage he discussed without having notes in front of him. These explications were based on years of studying the Bible, but the delivery method was different from writing commentaries. These lectures were transcribed, most likely by one of the students, and then published. Later republications of Calvin's works, however, often do not distinguish between the commentaries and the lectures, and both types of works are considered Calvin's Bible commentaries.

The following are the commentaries that Calvin published, in chronological order: Romans (1540); 1 and 2 Corinthians (1546, with a new edition of 1 Corinthians published in 1556); Galatians, Ephesians, Philippians, and Colossians (1548); 1 and 2 Timothy (1548); Hebrews (1549); Titus (1550); James (1550); 1 and 2 Thessalonians as well as Philemon printed together with the commentaries on all the epistles of Paul and the epistle to the Hebrews (1551); James, 1 and 2 Peter, 1 John, and Jude (1551); Isaiah (1551, expanded edition 1559); Acts 1–13 (1552); the Gospel of John (1553); Acts 14–28 (1554); Genesis (or the First Book of Moses, 1554); Matthew, Mark, and Luke (or Harmony of the Gospels, 1555); Psalms (1557); Exodus to Deuteronomy, with the book of Genesis, printed together (1563); and Joshua (published by Beza after Calvin's death in 1564).

Calvin's lectures that were published as books are Hosea (1557); the Minor Prophets (1559); Daniel (1561); and Jeremiah and Lamentations (1563). Calvin delivered a series of lectures on Ezekiel toward the end of his life. He gave his last lecture on Ezekiel 20:44 on February 2, 1564, and after that he was too weak to lecture.

In What Way Did Calvin's Study of the Law Shape His Theology?

While Calvin indeed spent a few years of his life studying law, he never practiced law or worked as a lawyer, though some people mistakenly call him a lawyer. As discussed above, the education that Calvin received was deeply rooted in the spirit and viewpoint of early sixteenth-century humanism. This means that Calvin's studies included the reading of classical authors, the Greek philosophers, the early Christian authors such as Augustine and the Cappadocian Fathers, and many others. He also studied the medieval thinkers such as Thomas Aquinas, Peter Lombard, and others. In all, he was immersed in theology, philosophy, and the liberal arts. These areas of study gave him a wide and deep foundation for his own theological thoughts.

But the legal training that Calvin received at Orléans and at the University of Bourges did benefit him in his ministry as he led the church in Geneva, informing his views and approaches to marital laws, punishment of crimes, and protection of people's property. His deep understanding of the law also helped him craft the shape of the Consistory and its approach to various cases of wrongdoing. The close relationship but also distinct responsibilities of the church and the city council of Geneva were, in a way, the fruit of Calvin's deep roots in the knowledge of the law. He tried to balance between the law of the land and the teaching of the church in his ministry in Geneva. He had a rocky start when he first came to Geneva, but after a long while, he was able to implement most of his vision in the life of the city.

The most notable influence of Calvin's training in the law, in my opinion, was how it shaped his theological reflection. His explanation of salvation, which includes both justification and sanctification, is a great example of this. For him, our salvation starts with justification, by which God declares, on account of the righteousness of Christ imputed to us, that he no longer sees us as sinners but as justified people. Instead of having a God as a judge, he wrote, we have a Father who loves us so much that we receive pardon for our sins. Justification is God's decision (or declaration) that we are no longer sinners but freed people. This declaration is given once and for all by the judge, and therefore no more punishment is imposed on us. The punishment has been performed by Christ on the cross. He has taken our place, that of condemned sinners, so we can be free. In our salvation, Christ has done the work of an advocate who defends us and covers us with his blood of righteousness. As people who have been declared justified by God, we stand before him as free people. And because God is the one declaring our pardon, we are eternally justified. Sanctification is the process through which we work by the power of the Holy Spirit to live as God's children and to glorify him in our lives. In this explanation, you can see that he used legal categories and terms, including a judge, the declaration of pardon that the judge makes, and Christ who acts as our advocate.[8]

Calvin's explanation of the doctrine of God is also partly rooted in his study of the law. He employed vocabulary from the legal world to explain God's goodness and his judgment. In his explication of God as Creator and ruler of the universe, he showed that when God administers his sovereignty over all humans, he pours out his sovereign kindness to the people by giving clemency to the godly and severity to the wicked. In discussing the justice and mercy of God, Calvin always kept these two aspects of God's action together. God's justice is shown to those who stand against his Word, even if they go unpunished temporarily. His mercy, on the other hand, is demonstrated when he pursues sinners with undeterred kindness.[9] Through his mercy, God displays his goodness as

---

[8]Calvin, *Institutes* III.11.1.
[9]Calvin, *Institutes* I.5.7.

protector and vindicator of the innocent, bestower of all blessings, provider of their needs, and healer of their pains.

How Did Calvin's Understanding of Church, State, and Society Differ from Those of Other Christian Traditions?

As we have seen, in his own life and ministry, Calvin had a complicated relationship with the government of Geneva. Many of the Protestant Reformers worked with local government officials or magistrates as they sought to reform the church, which has earned them the moniker *Magisterial Reformers*. But exactly how this relationship played out varied. For example, Luther saw Christians in the world as living in two kingdoms: the worldly kingdom and the spiritual kingdom under Christ. This allowed him to work with state officials while at the same time maintaining the priority of people's spiritual lives. During the English Reformation, the establishment of the Church of England with Henry VIII as the head of the church made the state heavily involved in church matters, a view technically known as an Erastianism. By contrast, the Anabaptists detached themselves entirely from the state, looking at the church only as the holy community, which earned them the label *Radical Reformers*.

In Calvin's ministry, the spheres of the church and the state were related but distinct. His way of relating the two by employing the consistorial government of the church, which was closely connected to but distinct from the city council of Geneva, made his approach unique. Calvin believed that governments are given by God for the good of the people to ensure that people can live peacefully, that wrongdoers are punished, and that justice is maintained. As the people must obey the government, in return the government must do the work that God places upon it. The first important task is to ensure that the worship of the true God can always take place. With this theological view of the relationship between church and government, Calvin moved forward with implementing it in the city of Geneva. Even though his relationship with the Genevan city council was rocky at the beginning, later in his ministry he saw the fruit of his labor. He ably bridged the two institutions while placing the responsibilities of each within its own sphere. Matters pertaining to church and the spiritual lives of the people were the responsibilities of the church. The right to impose church discipline and to forbid people from the Lord's Supper when they are excommunicated, for instance, belonged to the church, not the city council. Punishment for crimes, on the other hand, was the responsibility of the city council.

Calvin was supportive of the close relationship between church and state, but he emphasized that the two institutions are not to be mixed into one. He had a strong voice in the government of Geneva, but he clearly maintained that his job was to be the pastor of the church. He had a close relationship with the syndics and other members of the Genevan city council, working together for the good of the community without confusing the two.

How Did Calvin's Theology of Saving Grace Lead Him to Get Involved in Mundane Matters of Life?

Calvin explains that God's grace of salvation brings us a double gift, namely justification and sanctification. Sanctification is inseparable from justification in that God's children strive to follow his Word and be obedient to the heavenly Father. Sanctification is a process that continues throughout our lives and is enabled by God's grace. The good work we do is an expression of gratitude given to God because he has saved us, not a condition for our salvation.

One way to answer this question is by looking at Calvin's explanation of the Ten Commandments, especially the second table of the law. Calvin explains that when the commandment is negative ("You shall not . . ."), the other side, the positive meaning of the

commandment, is equally important. For instance, the commandment "You shall not murder" means that we are not just to
refrain from taking the life of others, but we are called to do as
much as we can to help other people's lives to flourish. The practical
applications of this commandment are wide and varied. You can
think of a call to be a physician or a nurse as your way to fulfill the
commandment. The work of a police officer to protect people's lives
and wellbeing also fulfills this commandment. Another example is
the application of the commandment, "You shall not bear false
witness against your neighbor." Using this commandment, Calvin
reminds us that we keep the good names of others not only by not
telling lies or gossiping, but more than that, we are to appreciate
the goodness of others, be joyful in their achievements, and share
good news about others.

What Was Calvin's Attitude Toward People of Different Ethnic Origins or Different Faiths?

To understand Calvin's attitude toward people who came from
outside his circle, we first need to appreciate his approach to and
treatment of refugees in Geneva during his lifetime. He insisted
that Geneva provide a safe place for refugees, most of whom came
to the city because of religious persecution. The population of
Geneva was about ten thousand people before Calvin came, and as
religious exiles from Italy, Spain, the Low Countries, and other
parts of Europe came to Geneva, it reportedly doubled by the time
Calvin died. The 1541 Ecclesiastical Ordinances stipulated that the
hospital give aid not just to the sick but also to the aged, the
widowed, and the orphaned, as well as offer a place to stay for those
who were sojourning. Physicians and surgeons were to be employed
by the city to provide service for people, including refugees.

We can also answer this question by exploring Calvin's relationship with Jewish people. When Calvin arrived in Geneva in

1536, there were no longer any Jews in the city because they had been banished from Geneva and the surrounding region in 1491, as happened in other regions at that time. Therefore, Calvin never had direct contact with the Jews in Geneva. He may have had contact with them in Strasbourg, Frankfurt, and Ferrara, but he never wrote directly about an actual meeting with Jews. Calvin wrote one tract about the Jews, *Ad quaestiones et obiecta Judaei cuiusdam responsio,* or *Response to the Questions and Objections of a Certain Jew.* This tract was published in 1575, long after Calvin's death. The body of the work, which seemed to be unfinished, appeared in the form of questions and answers. In the dialogue, Calvin provided answers to the questions posed by the interlocutor. It aims at providing clarifications of Christian beliefs to the Jewish people; that is, it is intended to be a theological work. Stephen Burnett has argued that Calvin's interlocutor in this work was not an imaginary person, nor was Calvin writing in a different persona to represent the Jews, but the author of a work titled *Sefer Nizzahon,* or *The Book of Victory,* a work published in Germany sometime in the fourteenth century. It was an anthology of Jewish polemical works that already had a negative reputation among Christians long before the Reformation.[10] Calvin's reply to the author of *Sefer Nizahon,* therefore, was an expression of his thought about the Jews' objections to Christianity, not about the Jewish people living in Europe during this time.

Calvin's views regarding the Jews are hotly debated among Calvin scholars. There is still no clear consensus on exactly what he thought about them. In his lectures on the book of Daniel, Calvin once stated that he had some conversations with Jews and had a strong opinion against their religious beliefs. This may reflect the

---

[10]Stephen Burnett, "Calvin's Jewish Interlocutor: Christian Hebraism and Anti-Jewish Polemics During the Reformation," *Bibliothèque d'Humanisme et Renaissance* 55, no. 1 (1993): 113-23.

strong anti-Jewish view of Christians in his time. However, some
scholars argue that in his exegetical works, Calvin broke from the
anti-Jewish sentiments of his contemporaries and predecessors.
His exegetical approaches to some key biblical verses regarding the
Jews give us a more positive way of looking at Christian and Jewish
relations compared to similar works up to his time.[11] Calvin calls
the Israelites of the Old Testament God's people, showing that they
were members of the true church, but he also states that the Israelites—or the Jews—who are saved in Christ are the true remnant,
and not all receive salvation.

> Calvin's views on the Jews often reflected similar views
> held by his contemporaries. But a careful examination of his
> exegetical works also reveals that he is more positive than
> others in seeing the relationship between Christians and
> Jews. Emphasizing the unity of the covenant in both the Old
> and the New Testaments, he believes that the biblical Jews
> were the people of God, the church, which God holds in his
> providential care.

Like many theologians of his day, Calvin never hesitated to use
strong language and harsh vocabulary when he defended his understanding of a true Christian belief against his opponents. The
leaders of the Church of Rome, the Anabaptists, the Libertines, and
many others received these strong words from Calvin. The Jews
who opposed Christianity did not receive different treatment from
Calvin. For him, the dividing line was the faithful interpretation of
the Bible and orthodox belief. Therefore, when Calvin vehemently
disagreed with the Jews, he should be understood from a

---

[11]Sujin Pak, "A Break with Anti-Judaic Exegesis: John Calvin and the Unity of the Testaments," *Calvin Theological Journal* 46, no. 1 (2011): 7-28.

theological standpoint and not from our contemporary idea of racism or, in the case of the Jewish people, anti-Semitism.

Similar to his view on Judaism, Calvin's way of looking at Islam was also informed by his Christology. In particular, because Muslims do not believe fundamental Christian tenets, including the belief that Jesus is the Son of God (a phrase that sounds blasphemous to Muslims) or in the saving power of Christ—among other things, such as the authority of the Bible and the doctrine of the Trinity—Calvin firmly rejected their views. He also saw Islam as a political threat to Christianity. During his lifetime, under Suleiman I "The Magnificent" (who reigned 1520–1566), the Ottoman Empire expanded its territory from the southeastern part of the Mediterranean to some parts of Europe. Regarding the Turks, Calvin wrote in the *Institutes* that even though they say that they proclaim God as the Creator of heaven and earth, they reject Christ as the Savior. To him, this was equal to idolatry.[12]

If One Agrees with Calvin's Theology, Does It Mean That the Person Agrees with Colonialization and Everything It Brought?

This is an important question, but it is problematic because it assumes either that Calvin directly caused colonialization or that contemporary Christians who agree with Calvin's theology are as guilty as groups responsible for colonializing parts of the world, for example, the Dutch who colonized South Africa, leading to apartheid. It is true and it must be acknowledged that some of the Europeans who took part in the colonization of Africa, Asia, and other parts of the world embraced Calvin's theology. However, their motivation to colonize was to gain wealth and power over other people by exploiting them. They were not driven primarily by theological motives. As we know, unfortunately, other European groups

---

[12]Calvin, *Institutes* II.6.4.

who were part of different branches of Christianity also colonized other parts of the world. The Spaniards and the Portuguese were Roman Catholics, and they colonized many parts of South America and some parts of Asia. Though it was sometimes misused or abused during colonization, religion was not its driving force, so to connect religion—or Calvin and Calvinism—to colonization misses the target.

I am originally from Indonesia, and in the seventeenth century most of the region that is now Indonesia was under the power of the Dutch, who happened to be followers of the teachings of Calvin. Because of that, Calvinism took a reasonably strong hold in the region, and I am a beneficiary of this historical connection. While colonialization has a terrible history that inflicted great suffering and cannot be ignored, it has nothing to do with Calvin's theology. Rather, it has a lot to do with human sinfulness that manifested itself as greed, hunger for power, and often racism.

How Did Calvin's Teaching Spread All Over Europe and the Rest of the World?

The effects of Calvin's ministry and theology reached far beyond the city walls of Geneva. We have already seen, for example, that he ministered for some time in Strasbourg. But his work influenced many other regions too. For example, Calvin's theology is often associated with the French Huguenots, the churches in the Netherlands and Scotland, the Transylvanian Reformed congregations, Korean Presbyterian churches, and Presbyterian churches in North America. Christians in these and other regions around the world have benefited from Calvin's understanding of Scripture, his theology, and the way that he encouraged godly living in Geneva.

A few factors worked together to enable the spread of Calvin's teaching. In his lifetime, he made many contacts with people all over Europe, both politically and ecclesiastically, and naturally these contacts sparked the spread of his influence to different regions. Some of the people who sought refuge in Geneva later returned to their places of origin, and naturally they brought what they learned from Geneva to these places. Refugees from the Low Countries to London, for instance, developed a church community that embraced Calvin's theology. When they returned home and the political landscape changed, Calvinistic churches started to form there. In Scotland, the influence of Calvin's theology came through the work of John Knox, who had visited Calvin in Geneva. Scottish churches, while taking a different approach in terms of church government, are deeply rooted in Calvin's teaching. In England, following the accession of Elizabeth I to the throne, Calvin's theology found support. Later, Puritans in England adopted Calvin's theology, further spreading Calvin's influence not just in England but also into the New World as many of the Puritans sailed to the Americas.

During his lifetime, Calvin did not have much contact with people in the Netherlands; we have very few letters from Calvin to the people in the Low Countries. Yet in the second half of the 1540s, the Evangelicals or Protestants in the Low Countries experienced a significant amount of persecution, and many fled the country. Calvin's care for the Dutch in exile became the source of later close affiliation between the Low Countries and his teachings. A robust growth of the acceptance of Calvin's theology happened after the Dutch Revolt of 1566, two years after Calvin's death, and the Evangelicals openly established churches that adopted Calvin's teachings. They also adapted the ecclesial practices of Geneva in the Reformed churches that they established in the Low Countries.

Later, the nineteenth century saw the further spread of Calvin's thought through the work of Abraham Kuyper, a Dutch pastor, theologian, politician, journalist, and educator. He began his career as a pastor, then became an editor of two journals, and then founded a democratic party in the Netherlands, which led to his rise as the Prime Minister of the Netherlands from 1901 to 1905. Also a champion of education, he started the Free University of Amsterdam. Kuyper expanded the Reformed—or Calvinistic—worldview by emphasizing that all life is subjected under the lordship of Christ and dedicated for the glory of God. His six Stone Lectures, delivered at Princeton in 1898, have been published in English under the title *Lectures on Calvinism*.[13] Kuyper is commonly called the founder of Neo-Calvinism, a newer way of looking at Calvin's teachings, especially on how Christians apply their faith in all areas of life.

The subsequent generations of Reformed thinkers after Calvin developed their thoughts well beyond Calvin's own writings. While agreeing with many teachings of Calvin, they also expanded their theologies based on their understanding of Christianity and their interpretation of the Bible. Therefore, these Reformed theologians did not just parrot everything that Calvin wrote. As with every new generation, there were nuances and expansions of theological reflection that they added to the conversation. Today, when we use the terms *Calvinists* or *Reformed*, that does not entail agreeing with everything that Calvin wrote or practicing everything that Calvin did in the church of Geneva. In fact, Calvin himself understood that as his influence spread wider in Europe, different approaches to theology would develop based on each people's or church's circumstances. He certainly did not want people to make an idol of him.[14]

---

[13]Abraham Kuyper, *Lectures on Calvinism* (New York: Cosimo Classics, 2009).

[14]See Andrew Pettegree, "The Spread of Calvin's Thought," in *The Cambridge Companion to John Calvin*, ed. Donald K. McKim (Cambridge: Cambridge University Press, 2004), 207.

Suggestions for Further Reading

Billings, J. Todd, and John Hesselink, eds. *Calvin's Theology and Its Reception: Disputes, Developments, and New Possibilities*. Louisville, KY: Westminster John Knox, 2012.

Joustra, Jessica R., and Robert J. Joustra. *Calvinism for a Secular Age: A Twenty-First-Century Reading of Abraham Kuyper's Stone Lectures*. Downers Grove, IL: IVP Academic, 2022.

Murdock, Graeme. *Beyond Calvin: The Intellectual, Political, and Cultural World of Europe's Reformed Churches, c. 1540–1620*. New York: Palgrave McMillan, 2004.

Pak, Sujin. *The Judaizing Calvin: Sixteenth-Century Debates over the Messianic Psalms*. New York: Oxford University Press, 2010.

Tuininga, Matthew J. *Calvin's Political Theology and the Public Engagement of the Church: Christ's Two Kingdoms*. Cambridge: Cambridge University Press, 2017.

- 4 -

Calvin as a Pastor

The Pastor and the Church

We often think of Calvin as a theologian because he left us with a vast number of biblical commentaries and theological writings, most importantly the *Institutes*. However, we need to remember that Calvin wrote all his exegesis and theological teaching for the good of the church. In his heart of hearts, he was a servant of and shepherd to God's people. He wanted the congregation to have true knowledge of God and his Word, so he spent most of his energy trying to ensure that the people of God lived according to God's teaching in the Bible. In other words, Calvin was a pastor first and a theologian second. His strong convictions often put him at odds with his opponents, but amid all the challenges, he clearly wanted God's people to receive good spiritual nourishment and guidance as they journeyed in the world. In the preface to his commentary on the book of Psalms, he reflects on the similarity between David and himself. God called David with all his struggles and short-comings to be God's instrument in leading Israel and also in writing the Psalms.[1] I happen to think that Calvin saw himself also as a shepherd who took care of sheep, sometimes in the quiet and

---

[1] John Calvin, "Preface," in *Commentary on the Psalms* (Edinburgh: Calvin Translation Society, 1845), 1:xxxix-xl.

beauty of green pastures but often in the face of beasts—enemies and adversaries.

The worshiping community. As a pastor, one of Calvin's primary duties and desires was to establish and enable true worship of God. To that end, he wanted the people to leave behind their old habits and theological beliefs shaped by the medieval church and culture and enter into a new way of life in light of the teaching and beliefs of the Reformation. As you can imagine, even though the church in Geneva had put the Ecclesiastical Ordinances in place in 1541, change took time. It was hard for people to shed their habits, ways of thinking, and established behaviors. In his role as a pastor, Calvin strove to ensure that this change happened. He often faced resistance from the people, partly because they were unwilling to change and partly because they were unsure of what change would look like. He did his part by teaching, preaching, writing, and sometimes imposing discipline. In the process, people sometimes misunderstood him as a tyrant. But as a shepherd to the sheep, he believed that he had to direct the sheep to take the right path, otherwise they would be in danger.

At the heart of worship in Geneva was exposure to the Word of God. Calvin preached almost every day of the week. On Sundays, he often preached twice. People were expected to go to church at least twice a week, once on Sunday and again on Wednesday. Calvin's intention was that people receive knowledge of God and his Word. This is in line with the spirit of the Reformation that Luther emphasized. The principle of *sola Scriptura*, or "Scripture alone," does not just mean that we are justified—and therefore receive redemption from sin—through Scripture. These come only from God's grace through Christ. But Scripture is God's Word for God's people, which nourishes, encourages, and sometimes chastens them. In the first line of the *Institutes*, Calvin wrote that all wisdom lies in the knowledge of God and knowledge of self. This statement has perhaps become the most quoted line from the *Institutes*. Calvin's emphasis on people having the true knowledge of God appears to be the underlying foundation of his pastoral work.

Calvin's significance as a pastor in reforming the church goes beyond the theological teachings that he advanced during his lifetime. His work in renewing the church's worship was equally important. Similar to what Luther and other first-generation Reformers did, Calvin brought worship into the mother tongue of the people—in this case, French. This included the entire liturgy, the preaching of the Word of God, and singing. Before the Reformation, there was very little congregational participation when people went to church. The focus of the people in the medieval era was the Mass, when they received the body and the blood of Christ. Other than receiving the sacrament, the people did not have much of a place in the liturgy of the church. Moreover, they often didn't understand what was being said or what was happening during worship. The priest spoke in Latin, the chants were in Latin, and the choirs sang in Latin.

In the Protestant churches after the Reformation, the congregation actively took part in worship. One example of this is singing. Martin Luther was known to be a hymn writer; his many hymns include the famous "A Mighty Fortress Is Our God." Similarly, Calvin also worked hard to bring congregational singing into the church. In fact, many Reformation scholars think that one of the biggest contributions Calvin made to the Reformation was his insistence that the church sing the metrical psalms in French.

Calvin believed that singing in church was a form of prayer. In the preface to his psalter published June 10, 1543, he explicitly mentioned that Christians can pray in two ways: through words, the typical form of prayer, but also through songs.[2] He believed that singing can move our hearts deeply so that through song we praise God and adore him dearly. Calvin also reminded people that the songs chosen to sing to God must be selected to be God-honoring, not just for our own human entertainment. In this way, he thought, the church could distinguish between songs that Christians sing at dinners or other social events and those sung at church in the presence of God. Singing at church also has the function of edifying the people in the truth of God's words.

Calvin held that the psalms were the best songs to use to sing and to pray to God in worship. He believed that they are honest and holy expressions of our prayers. They rouse in the hearts and minds of believers a willingness to praise God and to meditate on his goodness, so that they love, fear, honor, and glorify him at all times. Calvin believed that the church could use the words God has already given in the Psalms in the Bible, so the church didn't need to find songs elsewhere. Following Saint Chrysostom, Calvin declared that when the church sings, the whole people are in the company of angels in praising God in heaven. The melodies for the psalms, he reminded people, must be adjusted so that they support the majesty and the weightiness of the message of the psalms. God has created human bodies beautifully, and our tongues are created to speak and sing praises to God. In the *Institutes* he wrote that when people sing together at church, they sing with one voice as though they sing with just one mouth, to worship God in one spirit and in one faith.[3]

---

[2]This preface was often included in later publications of the Genevan psalter. See, for instance, *Les Pseaumes mis en rime francoise par Clément Marot et Théodore de Béze* (Lyon: Ian de Tournes, 1563), A2 recto–A5 verso.

[3]John Calvin, *Institutes of the Christian Religion* [1559], ed. John T. McNeill, trans. Ford Lewis Battles (Philadelphia: Westminster, 1960), III.20.31.

Figure 4.1. First stanza of Psalm 1 from *La Forme des prieres et chantz ecclesiastiques*, 1542

The sacraments also played a key role in the worshiping life of Calvin's church. Believing that the sacraments are the sign and the seal of God's covenant with his people, he viewed baptism as working rather similarly to the circumcision of Abraham's descendants as children of the covenant. Just as the baby boys, in being circumcised at eight days old, received the sign of God's covenant, baptism given to children marks the same covenant for children of believing parents, though importantly both infant boys and girls could be baptized. Holding the significance of the Lord's Supper for Christians highly, Calvin insisted that the church in Geneva should have a frequent celebration of the sacrament. He always believed that although the sacraments were not necessary for salvation, they were needed to support and uphold the faith of the people. Without the sacraments, their faith might easily collapse. As a pastor, he wanted the Genevans to be nourished spiritually by the body and blood of Christ through weekly celebrations of the Lord's Supper. But the resistance he received from the Genevan city council at that time was very strong. They wanted less frequent observance of the sacrament. The issue of the Lord's Supper and other struggles caused him to be deposed from Geneva in 1538. When he eventually returned to Geneva in 1541, he returned to the task of shepherding the sheep and leading God's people in the proper worship of God.

Pastoral care amid suffering. Another primary duty of the pastor is providing pastoral care even in extremely difficult circumstances. The plague hit the Swiss Confederation starting in 1542, and it reached Geneva and the surrounding areas in 1543. The city of Geneva took care of the people suffering from the plague in a hospital outside of the city, and the sick needed spiritual and pastoral care from the ministers in Geneva. However, as we can imagine, it was dangerous for the ministers to visit the sick, because they could easily contract the plague as well. Many of the ministers in Geneva were reluctant to go, and only three volunteered, namely Calvin, Sebastian Castellio, and Peter Blanchet. They decided to cast lots, and Castellio was selected. But he changed his mind and said he did not want to go anymore. Calvin volunteered himself, but the city council prevented him from going because they thought he was needed to lead the church in Geneva. Therefore, Blanchet volunteered to carry out the task of caring for the sick. Sadly, however, he later died because of the plague.

Calvin was deeply concerned when the plague swept over Geneva and its vicinity. The plague was still lingering in the area in 1545. In September of that year, he wrote a letter to Farel to express his worries.[4] In the letter he stated that a minister by the name of Mathaeus was busy working for the sick at the hospital, and another minister, Louis de Geniston, whom he called a dear colleague, had just died. De Geniston followed the bravery of Blanchet to volunteer to go to the hospital. After his death, his wife and two of their children also died because of the plague. Calvin feared that other ministers would die because of the plague. He was concerned that the ministers serving the sick due to the plague would be locked in without any means to survive. As a pastor, Calvin had to juggle between ministering to the congregation in Geneva and taking care of the sick who were in the hospital outside of the city. This was a real struggle for a pastor, but Calvin sought to remind the people of God's faithfulness even in dire situations.

Education of God's people. Another aspect of Calvin's view of his calling is the value he placed on the edification and education of all people, especially the young. He wrote several editions of the catechism in both French and Latin during his ministry in Geneva, all for the specific purpose of instructing young people with the basic knowledge of the Christian faith. By writing the catechism in French, he would reach readers more easily, especially children and those living in Geneva. However, the catechisms written in Latin could reach an audience beyond Geneva. He wanted the Latin edition of the catechism, published in 1545, to be used as a tool to

---

[4]John Calvin, "Letter CXLVIII," in *Letters of John Calvin*, ed. Jules Bonnet (New York: B. Franklin, 1973), 2:22-23.

unify all the churches that accepted his view. Even though the churches were geographically separated from each other, by having one catechism in the language that was common to most people, the churches were able to learn the same faith. The Latin catechism would be easily translated into other languages to be used by churches throughout Europe. In fact, Beza wrote that soon after its publication, the catechism was translated into several languages, including German, English, Scottish, Flemish, Spanish, and surprisingly enough, even Hebrew (by Emmanuel Tremmelius) and Greek (by Henry Stephen).

On the church and its ministers. In his reflections on the nature of the church, Calvin discussed two versions of the church. The first is the church of God's people all over the world—since the creation of the world until the second coming of Jesus. These are the people God calls and gathers to be his people through his eternal decree of election. Jesus died for them, and through his death they receive redemption. This invisible or universal church is the church that is meant in the affirmation of the Nicene Creed: "We believe in one, holy, catholic, and apostolic church." In its universality, this church exists across boundaries of time and place.

The second version of the church is the church that exists in a time and place as an institution. Theologically, Calvin kept both churches in his view, but his real work was for the church of his own time in a definite location—the city of Geneva. The members of this so-called visible church are people who lived their lives, worshiped, and worked in the city. From Calvin's theological viewpoint, not all the members of the visible church are members of the invisible or universal church. Jesus' parable of the wheat and the tares explains this (Mt 13:24-30). The wheat are the true members of the universal church, and the tares are not. But temporarily, the wheat and the tares grow together in the same field. When applied to the visible church, the parable carries the message that both groups of people exist side by side. They go to church together, they live in the same city, and they interact with each other regularly. But some members of the visible church may not be members of the invisible church. Calvin was clear that it was not his job—nor ours—to say which one is which. Only God knows his elect people. Calvin knew that his task as a pastor was to take care of the people without trying to distinguish them. He demanded that all Genevans live as Christians truthfully, leaving behind lives of immorality and sin and pursuing holy living as God's people.

Calvin required a high standard from all the other pastors who worked in the church in Geneva. The church, therefore, established the Company of Pastors, which governed the duties and the lives of the pastors. Appealing to Ephesians 4:11-12, "the gifts he gave were that some would be apostles, some prophets, some evangelists, some pastors and teachers, to equip the saints for the work of ministry, for building up the body of Christ," Calvin insisted that teaching and preaching the Word of God faithfully was the foremost way pastors carry out their duties. To put what Paul wrote in Ephesians 4 into practice, the Ecclesiastical Ordinances of 1541 outline four offices in the church: pastors, teachers, elders, and deacons. The church order has long regulations and guidelines on how ministers must perform their work and how they must behave as God's servants. They include a description of the duties of pastors, the selection criteria and examination of candidates, the acceptable and unacceptable conduct of pastors, and the disciplinary actions for a pastor's failure to do his duty or keep good conduct. These rules were applied to all pastors whether they served in the urban or rural churches in Geneva. In the city of Geneva itself, there were three churches, Sainte-Pierre, Sainte-Gervais, and La Madeleine. In addition, there were several rural churches in the villages just outside of the city walls. By following these standards, Calvin sought to provide the people of God with faithful shepherds.

The Pastor and the Consistory in Geneva

As mentioned above, the Consistory was formed in the city of Geneva to guide the people to live as upright Christians. Calvin insisted on the Consistory as a condition of his 1541 return, and the Ecclesiastical Ordinances secured the founding of such a Consistory. Once it was established, the Consistory met once a week, on Thursdays. On the week leading to Communion, it had an additional meeting on Tuesday.[5] The meeting of the Consistory was chaired by a syndic, with twelve elders of the church and all the urban ministers attending. Having the syndic preside ensured that the Consistory sessions were the affairs of both the secular government and the church. People were called to appear before the Consistory when there were moral or ecclesial issues. The cases brought before the Consistory varied widely, including adultery and fornication, fights and quarrels, domestic violence, marriage and divorce, theft, drunkenness, and everything in between. But perhaps the most important issue that the church in Geneva dealt with was ensuring that people went to church regularly. Regular church attendance, the Consistory argued, would naturally lead to a changed worldview. Calvin and the Geneva Consistory expected that worship would change the people's understanding of God, the sacraments, and life as a whole. In addition, it continually emphasized the people's need to know the basic beliefs of the church expressed in the Lord's Prayer and the Apostles' Creed. Calvin seemed to see this last point as a good indicator that the people had reached a benchmark of truly following the Word of God. When the people went to church faithfully and listened to sermons

---

[5]The transcription of most of the registers of the Consistory at the time of Calvin is now available in multiple volumes in French published by Droz in Geneva. The first volume of the register, covering the years 1542–1544, has been translated and published in English. Prof. Robert Kingdon and several other scholars who were formerly his students have been working hard to publish the registers. For this English translation, see Robert M. Kingdon et al., eds., *Registers of the Consistory of Geneva in the Time of Calvin* (Grand Rapids, MI: Eerdmans, 2000).

carefully, they would gain a deeper knowledge of the Word of God. Furthermore, the visible behavior of Protestant Christians would hasten the people's departure from previous practices. This meant that the people were forbidden to pray with the rosary or to pray to the saints. If someone was caught observing these old practices, that person would surely be called to appear before the Consistory.

Robert Kingdon explains that during a Consistory session, the syndic would conduct the interrogation with the ministers, mostly Calvin, interceding from time to time. A secretary would write down the conversation between the syndic and the person being questioned as much as possible. A session at the Consistory was usually started by the syndic, who had been informed of the problem or the wrongdoing someone was charged with. Once the interrogation was finished, the person was asked to leave the hall, and a witness or witnesses related to the case came to give their side of the explanation. When the Consistory was done with these proceedings, it would declare its sentence. In most cases, the Consistory would declare admonitions. In some serious cases the person would be excommunicated, which meant that the person was forbidden to partake in the Lord's Supper for a period of time until he or she repented. The most severe cases would merit a physical punishment, in which the Consistory sent the person to the city council to be sentenced.

FUN FACT

The Consistory was a collaboration between the Geneva city council and the church. The presence of the syndic signified the council's presence. However, in most cases, Calvin was the one taking the lead in interrogating the people.

The minutes of the Consistory sessions provide us with a wealth of information about what happened in Geneva during that time. They show us how the people struggled and stumbled as they tried to live as Christians and to keep up with the changes the Reformation brought. In the first two years the Consistory existed, there were 639 cases brought before that body involving 1,105 people. The minutes also give us a good window into Calvin's work as a pastor who wanted his congregation to be faithful Christians. In the early years of the Consistory, the majority of the cases concerned people's failures to attend church services regularly, their inability to say the prayer or creed correctly in French, or their engagement in religious practices that still reflected the medieval system. It is noteworthy that the Consistory called more women than men, most of whom were widows and mothers. Bruce Gordon aptly observes that the Consistory called mostly women because it saw the significance of women in the religious education of the youngsters in their houses.[6] For the Reformation to move forward, these women had central roles, and therefore they needed to have the foundational knowledge of Christianity so they could help bring change.

Some cases from the Consistory records provide insight into some of the challenges that Calvin faced in his work as a pastor. For instance, on Tuesday, March 20, 1543, Janne, the widow of Pierre Aprin, was called before the Consistory.[7] She was summoned because of the issue of superstition, namely that she was suspected of keeping medieval practices. She also skipped church services on a regular basis. She admitted that she had missed services a few times. However, on the day she appeared before the Consistory, she said that she had gone to church the previous Sunday. When asked who preached that Sunday, she said that she did not know the preacher. To make herself look better, she claimed that two Sundays before the previous one she went to church, and she firmly declared that

---

[6]Bruce Gordon, *Calvin* (New Haven, CT: Yale University Press, 2009), 135.

[7]Robert Kingdon, ed., *Registers of the Consistory of Geneva in the Time of Calvin*, vol. 1, *1542–1544* (Grand Rapids, MI: Eerdmans, 1996), 209.

Calvin was the preacher then. The same also happened in the case of Robellaz, the widow of Falcoz Vachon, who appeared before the Consistory on Thursday, November 22, 1543.[8] Even though she was called because she skipped church too frequently, she tried to put a good face before Calvin. She reasoned that even though she only went to church on Sundays and not on other days of the week, she remembered when Calvin preached. She then said that she even tried to remember the content of the sermon as much as she could. Such was the case with Anthoyne de Crouz, who appeared before the Consistory on Thursday March 15, 1543.[9] He stated that he went to church at La Madeleine and remembered Calvin's sermon on Joseph being sold by his brothers. Even though Anthoyne was summoned because of anger issues against his wife and his mother and not about the issue of infrequent church attendance, he took pride in remembering Calvin's sermon.

When Calvin did not preach on a given Sunday, people often did not remember who delivered the sermon at church when they attended those services. In those days, there were several ministers in Geneva, and they preached in turn each Sunday. Taverne, the widow of Marquet Peronet, appeared before the Consistory on Thursday, November 29, 1543.[10] She was called because of her relationships with various men. When the questioning turned to her church attendance, she stated that she went to church on Sundays. However, when she was questioned about who preached the previous Sunday, she only remembered that the preacher was a handsome man with a beard. Something similar also happened to Nycod de la Ravoyre the elder, who was called by the Consistory on Thursday, April 5, 1543.[11] He claimed that he went to hear the

---

[8]Kingdon, *Registers of the Consistory of Geneva*, 1:293.
[9]Kingdon, *Registers of the Consistory of Geneva*, 1:205.
[10]Kingdon, *Registers of the Consistory of Geneva*, 1:295.
[11]Kingdon, *Registers of the Consistory of Geneva*, 1:226.

sermons twice on Sundays, but when asked who preached the previous Sunday, he could not say the preacher's name, nor did he remember the main content of the sermon he heard.

Despite the slowness in change, Calvin's message indeed reached the minds of his congregation, even if one person at a time. We know of Claude Tappugnier, an ironmonger, who came before the Consistory on Thursday, April 5, 1543.[12] He seemed to be waffling between the medieval church's theology and that of the Reformation. He indicated that he still had theological uncertainties. He was alternating between his view of salvation as being either based on good works or by faith alone. He stated that he believed God was the one causing people to do good works, and therefore he did good works because of the grace of God. At the same time, he was still unsure whether he should pray to the Virgin Mary, as praying to the Virgin may constitute a good work. He was also questioning whether the Virgin could truly intercede on behalf of the people. At the end of the interrogation, he said that Calvin's explanations had relieved him from some of the doubts he had.

Some people challenged Calvin's authority as a pastor. Those who wanted to cling to their former religious practices sometimes looked on Calvin with contempt. For example, a noblewoman in Geneva by the name of Jane Pertennaz was summoned by the Consistory on Tuesday, March 20, 1543.[13] As a woman with high social status, she demonstrated an air of resistance to the Consistory and declared that she still did all the rituals that she had done before the changes of the Reformation happened, including praying with the rosary. Understanding that she was in a different time, she also said that she did not want to be called a heretic and that the church of Geneva was improved. However, toward the end of the interrogation, she boldly challenged Calvin and asked

---

[12]Kingdon, *Registers of the Consistory of Geneva*, 1:226
[13]Kingdon, *Registers of the Consistory of Geneva*, 1:211.

if he thought he was God. The woman was prohibited from partaking in the Lord's Supper the following Sunday because of her behavior. This incident illustrates the fact that some people in Geneva found it hard to accept the new order of the church under the leadership of Calvin.

Jane, the wife of Claude Pignier, presented a somewhat difficult problem to the ministers in Geneva. She was an Anabaptist and had been imprisoned and banished from Geneva in 1537. Her neighbors requested that the city council allow her to return, as she was able to teach their children. The request was granted, and she returned to the city in June of 1538. However, once back in Geneva, she did not cease causing trouble. On Thursday December 27, 1544, she was summoned by the Consistory.[14] The charges directed at her concerned issues including her view of infant baptism, her participation in Communion, and her conformity to the rules of the Reformed church in Geneva. She gave long answers to the questions, and during her answer she showed that she favored Pierre Viret over Calvin by implying that the latter was not a good pastor. The Consistory reported that she had called him a persecutor and a false prophet. However, when she was confronted, she denied ever saying that. At that session Calvin directly asked the Consistory to give the woman a chance to speak her mind, specifically to ask her what harm he had done to her. Her response was that she was not happy to be called before the Consistory, because in her opinion the Consistory was made to punish fornication, something she was not guilty of. This incident gives us some insight into the challenges Calvin faced as a pastor. Then, as now, the work of the pastor is often not about significant theological debates but about shepherding the flock of God.

---

[14]Kingdon, *Registers of the Consistory of Geneva*, 1:312-13.

The Pastor and His Letters

Calvin's letters provide us with a window into his thoughts and ministry as a pastor. In his lifetime, he wrote numerous letters to colleagues, opponents, state leaders, kings, noblewomen, and other people in power. But he also wrote letters to ordinary church-goers. While the letters to leaders and influential people in his time give us the bigger picture of the spread of the Reformation in sixteenth-century Europe and how Protestant theology was ex-plained, codified, and debated, his letters to ordinary—and often suffering—people show us Calvin's heart as a pastor.

For example, when he was still in Strasbourg in April 1541, he learned about the death of the son of a certain Monsieur de Richen-bourg living in Regensburg.[15] He stated that he was grieved for days when he thought about the death. He knew de Richenbourg's son Louis, and he was very sad that a young man such as Louis had died prematurely. He admitted that grief was natural, and having to see a son taken away from his father because of death was painful. However, he also reminded him that God has the utmost authority over life and death, and therefore he should not blame God for the death of his son. He sought to strengthen his friend by telling him that God was sovereign over all situations, even death. He hoped that his letter could help ease de Richenbourg's sadness. He also asked Bucer and Melanchthon to write to de Richenbourg so that together, the three ministers could provide comfort to him. In writing this letter, Calvin demonstrated deep pastoral care to a grieving father. He balanced the acknowledgment of grief and the need for one to rely on God for help.

Calvin's concern for people's well-being and growth in faith is reflected in many of his letters. In one case, he sent a letter to a lady

---

[15]The letter is printed in Hugh T. Kerr, ed., *By John Calvin* (New York: Association Press, 1960), 93. The letter is taken from Calvin, *Letters of John Calvin*, 1:246-53.

whose name he did not mention. She had sent Calvin a modest sum of ten crowns for poverty relief in Geneva. As an expression of gratitude, Calvin wrote a rather long letter to her on January 12, 1549, thanking her and encouraging her to stay steadfast in her faith.[16] In the letter, he also stated that from time to time, God allows his people to go through difficulty, and sometimes our faith grows weary because of the challenges we face in life. However, God never leaves us. He then encouraged her to be fervent in prayers and to keep the flame of her faith in God burning. Such a letter to a woman who did not have a prominent place in society, but who had a kind heart to help the poor in Geneva, demonstrates Calvin's warmth in dealing with others.

Death always brings sorrow, and Calvin himself experienced his share of this sadness. As discussed, he lost his wife and child to death, and he often related on a very personal level to others who went through the same loss. Richard Vauville, a minister of the French church in Frankfurt, lost his wife because of the plague in November 1555.[17] Calvin acknowledged the deep wound that the death of his wife had caused him, and he understood that Vauville now experienced similar sorrow. He admitted that the sadness was real, but at the same time, he consoled his friend by reminding him that God takes care of all his people. As a comfort, he reminded his grieving friend that God will once again reunite all of us with our loved ones in his celestial kingdom. Richard Vauville died just one month after his wife's death, and Calvin wrote a letter to the congregation of the French church in Frankfurt to express his condolences and to show appreciation of what Vauville had done for the church there.

In Chambery, in the southeast part of France, five young men were imprisoned because of their Protestant beliefs. They had set

---

[16]Calvin, Letter CCXXXIII, in *Letters of John Calvin*, 2:206-7.
[17]Calvin, Letter CCCCXXI, in *Letters of John Calvin*, 3:236.

out from Geneva to spread the Reformed faith in Chambery, but they were arrested and imprisoned. Upon hearing the news, Calvin wrote a letter to these men on September 5, 1555.[18] He encouraged them to stay steadfast in their faith in God, he reminded them that their works for God would not be in vain, and he assured them that God would take care of them, both body and soul, in his eternal goodness. In a fashion characteristic of his writings, he ended the letter with a prayer that God would always keep them by the power of his Spirit. He also consoled them by saying that the whole church had been praying for them, so they were not alone in facing this persecution. The men replied to Calvin's letter, thanking him for his kindness and stating that they were ready to be martyred. They were honest about fearing death but also showed that they had total faith in God. Calvin replied on October 5, 1555.[19] He once again reminded them that God the Father would always take care of his children. He stated that he would do anything he could to help them, but the situation was such that it was not possible for him or others in Geneva to help release them from prison. He consoled them with words of Psalm 16:8 that they should cast their eyes on God even when people went against them and there seemed to be no help or defense for them. As usual, he ended the letter with a prayer for God to keep them in the power of his Holy Spirit.

Three days after he sent the letter to the five men in prison, Calvin wrote a letter to the leaders of the city of Chambery, a protest against the treatment of the young men and persecution of the Protestants.[20] He asked them to always be close to God in prayer and to repent to be on the side of God. He also warned them that if they thought that they could continue to do their work because of their

---

[18]Calvin, Letter CCCCXIII, in *Letters of John Calvin*, 3:220-21.
[19]Calvin, Letter CCCCXVIII, in *Letters of John Calvin*, 3:232.
[20]Calvin, Letter CCCCXIX, in *Letters of John Calvin*, 3:233-34.

own powers, Satan would attack and deceive them. Even in his obvious dissatisfaction in what the leaders of Chambery had done, Calvin still showed kindness to them as he ended the letter. He stated that he would continue to pray to God the Father that he would keep them safe, so that they could resist temptation, and that the Holy Spirit would guide them to take the right path.

France's persecution toward Protestants was not limited to men. The French leaders were not hesitant to imprison, torture, and martyr women too. In September 1557, several women and men in Paris were arrested. Beza reported that these women were abused and degraded. One of these women was Philippe de Lunz, the widow of Seigneur de Graveron. She was sentenced to death, and her execution took place on September 27, 1557. She faced the fire courageously, wrote Beza, and set a great example for other women who were still waiting for their execution. Calvin wrote a letter to these women in the same month.[21] He expressed his deep sorrow for them, but he reminded them that God works even through the most difficult situations. God was using them, he said, to demonstrate that women were as worthy as men to carry out his work. God was pleased, Calvin wrote, to call both men and women for his work, and therefore Calvin tried to strengthen their faith as they went through their persecution. He reminded them that God would equip them with courage and with the words necessary for them to face their enemies. Quoting the prophet Joel, he stated that God poured out the Holy Spirit for both men and women, and also for young and old people (Joel 2:28). He also retold the courage of the women surrounding the death of Jesus: when the apostles and other men hid, the women came out and were the first ones to witness the resurrection of Christ (Mt 28:1-10). Throughout history, women had devoted themselves to God, and many of them died for the

---

[21]Calvin, Letter CCCCLXXVI, in *Letters of John Calvin*, 3:364-66.

name of Christ, so they were not alone. God would always be with them, Calvin reminded them.

Calvin extended his pastoral attention to the Reformed churches all over Europe. He wrote to encourage them and to exhort them to continue to be faithful in the work of God, even when they faced challenges along the way. One example of such a letter was the one he sent to the Protestant church in Meaux. The congregation was the birthplace of the Reformed church in France, and its close proximity to Paris made it vulnerable. Despite the challenges coming from the Catholics in Paris, the Reformed congregation in Meaux continued to grow. In his letter to the church in Meaux, dated January 5, 1558, Calvin expressed his appreciation to the church. He stated that it was not easy for the church to continue standing amid the challenges. What the people needed to do was take up their strength and conform themselves more and more to the doctrine of Jesus Christ as they prayed fervently to God the Father. The church in Geneva also sent a minister to the church in Meaux to help them grow, so that they would continue to follow the lead of the Great Shepherd. Calvin's letter and his part in Geneva's action to help another church are further evidence that Calvin's pastoral work was wider than just the local congregation in Geneva. He had the church universal in view while working tirelessly for the local church in Geneva at the same time.

As mentioned previously, Calvin paid careful attention to the need for education in the faith. On one occasion, he wrote an encouraging letter to a Polish lady, Madame Agnes de Microw of Cracow, who sent her children to study in Zurich. He sent the letter from Geneva on December 29, 1554.[22] He acknowledged that it must have been exceedingly difficult for her to be separated from her children and to allow them to live and study in a foreign land.

---

[22]Calvin, Letter CCCLXXVII, in *Letters of John Calvin*, 3:112-13.

However, he encouraged her by affirming that the children had gone away for a worthy purpose, namely, to study the true doctrine of Christ. Therefore, he assured her that when she was reunited with her children again after they finished their studies, she would be fully delighted not only to see them again but also to know that they had advanced the true teaching of the Bible. He also comforted her by saying that the leaders of the church in Zurich would certainly take good care of her children so that she did not need to worry about their wellbeing. She had become a role model for other women, he added, not only because of her upright Christian character but also for her willingness to send her children to study in a different land for the benefit of the Protestant cause.

As a pastor, Calvin was also a champion in making contacts with people from all walks of life and connecting people with one another, building a wide web of Protestants all over Europe and using his connections for the good of others. He helped young people to get theological educations under notable teachers whom he knew in many parts of Europe. On August 15, 1556, Calvin wrote a letter to Rodolph Gualter, a well-respected pastor and professor in Zurich, on behalf of a young man who wanted to study under him.[23] The boy was the son of a senator, but the family did not have much money for the boy's education abroad. Calvin asked Gualter to teach the boy without charging too much for his tuition. Gualter's help would mean much not only for the boy but also for Calvin's relationship with the boy's parents, whom Calvin respected. He was confident that Gualter would respond positively to his request. In the same letter, he also related to Gualter the incident of the collapse of one of the spires of Sainté-Pierre due to a lightning strike the previous Monday. The damage on the roof of the church was serious, but Calvin was confident that God would help them in the

---

[23]Calvin, Letter CCCCXLI, in *Letters of John Calvin*, 3:289-90.

work of repairing the church. This letter gives us a glimpse of the intricateness of Calvin's work as a pastor. As he thought about the future and education of a young boy, he connected the boy to a famous teacher to be educated. At the same time, as a pastor he also had to deal with the damage and the repair of the church's roof, which would have been a great expense. As a pastor, Calvin's primary task was to lead God's people in the true knowledge and worship of God, but he sometimes had to wear different hats: comforter, persuader, encourager, fundraiser, and more.

Calvin's letters also demonstrate his willingness to speak his mind honestly and not to hold back when he perceived a compelling need to express his thoughts. This honesty sometimes led him to be perceived as a harsh person, both in his own time and afterward. One example of this comes from his relationship with Farel, who had pleaded and cajoled him to stay in Geneva to advance the work of the Reformation back in 1536. Farel was like a big brother to Calvin when the young leader was finding his way in the ministry of the church. Still, there were times when Calvin criticized his older friend. Farel was a faithful leader, but he was not a charismatic preacher. He acknowledged his weakness, but he seems to have done little to attempt to remedy this problem. Having observed Farel struggle with his preaching style for some time, Calvin wrote a letter to his older colleague and confidant on January 27, 1552.[24] In the letter, Calvin plainly stated that the long-windedness of Farel's sermons had been a topic of complaints from many people at church. At first, he said, the grumblings of the people were done in private. But lately there had been so many complaints that they were no longer isolated incidents. He pleaded with Farel to take action quickly, so that he would not give Satan the opportunity to cause trouble in the church. He reminded Farel that the Lord called

---

[24]Calvin, Letter CCXCI, in *Letters of John Calvin*, 2:337.

them to be pastors for the edification of the people. Therefore, he asked Farel to change his style of preaching so that the Word of God could be properly communicated to the people, and they would not be distracted by Farel's tedious way of delivering his sermons. In the same letter, he stated that Farel's lengthy prayers at church had become an issue. He was supportive of pastors praying long prayers privately at home. However, when leading prayers during worship services, brevity was preferable. Such a letter would not have been easy to write, but it was done for the benefit of the church.

Calvin's relationship with Farel went through an even more serious challenge when his older friend decided to remarry, proposing to a girl who was only about sixteen years old. Farel was sixty-nine and a widower at that time. He had provided shelter in his house to the girl, her widowed mother, and her brother. Calvin was horrified when Farel told him about the wedding plan in the summer of 1558. He charged Farel as a mentally unstable old man. Later that summer, Farel came to Geneva to ask for Calvin's support, but Calvin refused to provide it. Farel could not cancel the wedding because the marital banns had been made in the church. The summer wedding was postponed, but finally Farel married the young woman on December 20, 1558. For many years Calvin's friendship with Farel was severely damaged because of this marriage. The friendship was only mended when Farel visited Calvin on his deathbed a few days before Calvin died.

The ministry of a pastor is a serious matter and a high calling. In fulfilling his pastoral office, Calvin's primary focus was on bringing the Word of God to the people of God. He tirelessly preached, taught, lectured, wrote his biblical commentaries, wrote theological treatises, and developed catechisms to provide people with the true knowledge of God's Word. Calvin used everything that he could to fulfill his calling, including the Consistory, the Company of Pastors, and his personal and professional contacts. His letters also reveal his pastor's heart, which cried when people lost loved ones to deaths by illness or martyrdom. He was not willing to compromise the truth of the Bible or the principles of his pastoral calling, even when he had to part ways with an old friend as close as Farel. In all that he did, he put his love of God and the church at the center of his heart.

Suggestions for Further Reading

Godfrey, W. Robert. *John Calvin: Pilgrim and Pastor.* Wheaton, IL: Crossway, 2009.

Kingdon, Robert. *Adultery and Divorce in Calvin's Geneva.* Cambridge, MA: Harvard University Press, 1995.

Manetsch, Scott. *Calvin's Company of Pastors: Pastoral Care and the Emerging Reformed Church 1536–1609.* New York: Oxford University Press, 2013.

Mentzer, Raymond. *Sin and the Calvinists: Moral Control and the Consistory in the Reformed Tradition.* Kirksville, MO: Truman State University Press, 2002.

Pitkin, Barbara, ed. *Semper Reformanda: John Calvin, Worship, and Reformed Traditions.* Göttingen: Vandenhoeck & Ruprecht, 2018.

Selderhuis, Herman, and Arnold Huijgen, eds. *Calvinus Pastor Ecclesiae.* Göttingen: Vandenhoeck & Ruprecht, 2016.

Witte, John, Jr., and Robert Kingdon, eds. *Sex, Marriage, and Family in John Calvin's Geneva.* Vol. 1. *Courtship, Engagement, and Marriage.* Grand Rapids, MI: Eerdmans, 2005.

Part Two

A Guide to
INSTITUTES OF THE
CHRISTIAN RELIGION

- 5 -

Editions of *Institutes*
of the Christian Religion

The 1536 Edition of the *Institutes*

Calvin published the first edition of *Institutes of the Christian Religion* in Basel in 1536. He had arrived there in 1535, and he made many like-minded acquaintances. He completed the book in September 1535 and dedicated it to Francis I, King of France. At that time, it was a common practice for authors to dedicate their published books to influential individuals in society. Among authors' hopes were that the persons to whom the books were dedicated would agree with what they wrote, defend the causes presented by them, support their movements, or help them gain wider readership.

Calvin's intention in dedicating his book to Francis I was clear: Calvin wanted the king not only to defend the Evangelicals, or Protestants, who had been unjustly persecuted in France but also to know what the core beliefs of the Evangelicals were. In the decades following Luther's Reformation in the early sixteenth century, the term *Evangelicals* referred to people who separated themselves from the Church of Rome and largely followed the beliefs and practices of the newly formed churches. However, the term was not always clearly or equally understood by people, and that may have been the case with King Francis.

King Francis, who aligned himself with the Church of Rome, disagreed with the Evangelicals. Luther's Reformation had spread widely, and the German Lutherans were already established as one church group. But the king considered the Reformed churches to be as radical and as rebellious as the Anabaptists. In France, the Evangelicals—practically all of whom were neither Catholic nor German Protestants—were persecuted. Calvin's intention in dedicating the *Institutes* to Francis was to show the king that Calvin's movement was not the same as that of the Anabaptists. He wanted to demonstrate the distance between his cause, under which Christians could still be good citizens, and that of this radical group. He also pleaded with the king that the persecution against the Evangelicals—the people who truly followed the beliefs of the Reformation—be ended. He also wanted to show the king that the Evangelicals held to the beliefs of the one true holy, catholic, and apostolic church.

Calvin wanted Francis to understand that the *Institutes* contained the most fundamental knowledge of true religion—the beliefs that lead people to godliness. His fellow French citizens were his main audience. Being French, Calvin always had a special place in his heart for the people of his home country. Even later in his life, when he worked and ministered to the church in Geneva, he continued showing his attention and affection to the French. He knew that the people in France were hungry and thirsty for the teaching of Christ, and he intended for the *Institutes* to give them what they needed.

Interestingly, even though Calvin intended the book for the French people, he wrote the first edition of the *Institutes* in Latin, the theological language common across traditions and geographical locations. The book was published by Thomas Platter and Balthasar Lasius in March 1536. As was the custom of the day, the title of the book is quite long. In English it can be translated *Institutes of the Christian Religion embracing almost the whole sum of piety and whatever is necessary to know of the doctrine of salvation: a work most worthy to be read by all persons zealous for piety, and recently published.*[1] It is clear from this lengthy title that Calvin wants his readers to know and understand the truth of the gospel and what it means for their lives.

The original contents. The 1536 edition of the *Institutes* is a relatively short book with only six chapters. Because he intends it to be read as simple instruction for those who were serious about being Christians, Calvin follows the standard structure of catechetical material. The first four chapters explain what Christians must know in following Christ: the Ten Commandments, the Apostles' Creed, the Lord's Prayer, and the sacraments. In the last two chapters, the book turns more polemical. In chapter five, Calvin criticizes the five additional sacraments of the Church of Rome. He rejects confirmation, penance, ordination, marriage, and the last rites as sacraments. He ends the book by examining the nature of Christian freedom, the power of the church, and civil government. In the last chapter, Calvin offers his own views on these, and he also challenges the beliefs and practices of the church that he considers to be wrong.

In writing the first edition of the *Institutes*, Calvin follows the approach that Martin Luther had taken. In his *Small Catechism*, first published in 1529, Luther intended that the catechism be used to teach young children the basic knowledge of the Christian faith. He wanted the leaders of the household to instruct the young by using the catechism. It contains basic knowledge about the Ten Commandments, the Apostles' Creed, the Lord's Prayer, baptism,

---

[1]For an English translation of the 1536 edition of the *Institutes*, see John Calvin, *Institutes of the Christian Religion: 1536 Edition*, trans. Ford Lewis Battles (Grand Rapids, MI: H. H. Meeter Center for Calvin Studies and Eerdmans, 1975).

confession, and the Lord's Supper. Calvin clearly structures the 1536 edition of the *Institutes* similarly to Luther's development of the themes in his *Small Catechism*, especially in the flow of the content of the first four chapters.

In the first chapter, Calvin opens the discussion of the Ten Commandments, or "the Law" as he calls it, with his overarching framework for understanding Christianity—namely, the relationship between knowledge of God and knowledge of self. This way of opening the *Institutes* became a standard in all subsequent editions of the book. Calvin starts by showing that true wisdom consists of these two forms of knowledge. They are not to be separated, and one informs the other. We can only know who we are when we know who God is. Our knowledge of God gives us true knowledge of who we are: people created by God who fell into sin and are in deep need of salvation that only comes from God through Christ. The law shows us that God demands perfection from us, but given our sinfulness, we are never able to measure up according to God's standard. Therefore, no single person can save himself or herself from the wrath of God. In other words, we cannot be justified by doing good works or keeping the law of God. We are justified only by God's grace in Christ.

With that foundation in place, Calvin proceeds to show that true faith is not just believing that God exists but acknowledging that Christ has come to be the only Savior of sinful humanity. The Apostles' Creed teaches us the core belief of this Christian faith. From there, Calvin explains the right way of praying to God through the prayer that Jesus himself has taught us (Mt 6:5-15). Besides teaching the meaning of the Lord's Prayer, he also explains the proper practice of prayer, or how Christians must pray to God. In the chapter on the sacraments, he shows that he stands in the Augustinian way of understanding sacraments as visible signs of God's invisible grace toward us that seal God's promises on our hearts and minds. He consistently holds this definition of sacraments in all editions of the *Institutes*.

In criticizing Rome's standpoint on what he viewed as five additional and unnecessary sacraments, Calvin plainly calls those sacraments—confirmation, marriage, ordination, penance, and extreme unction (or the last rites)—false. Besides being the visible sign of God's good will toward us in our salvation, sacraments must also be the seal of God's covenantal promise to his people. In his mind and in light of his reading of Scripture, only baptism and the Lord's Supper fulfill those functions. Sacraments must be established by God, he maintains.

The last chapter of the 1536 edition of the *Institutes* demonstrates Calvin's view of what living as true Christians looks like. Having been justified by God and living in the light of the gospel, Christians can freely lead a life obedient to the Word of God. We keep the law of God as an expression of gratitude about what God has done for us. He criticized the Church of Rome, which put too great a burden on its people to follow the rituals and the regulations of the church. In his opinion, Rome created laws that it claimed were spiritual only to put a heavy yoke on the people, since those laws were not prescribed according to God's Word. The true power of the church, he insists, is whatever is used to build up the people (2 Cor 12:19). Calvin ends the book with a look at the relationship between the civil government and the church. This early, brief version of the *Institutes* became the foundation of a work that Calvin would return to and steadily expand throughout his career.

The 1539 Edition of the *Institutes*

In 1538, after he was forced to leave Geneva, Calvin stayed in Basel for a short time before he moved to Strasbourg. He started writing the second edition of the *Institutes* in Basel, but the book itself was published in Strasbourg by Wendelinum Rihelium. Like its first edition, the second edition of the *Institutes* was written in Latin. He wrote the foreword of this new edition on August 1, 1539. He quite extensively expanded the number of topics discussed. In the 1539 edition of the *Institutes*, he retained the original six chapters of the 1536 publication and then added eleven more chapters for seventeen in total.

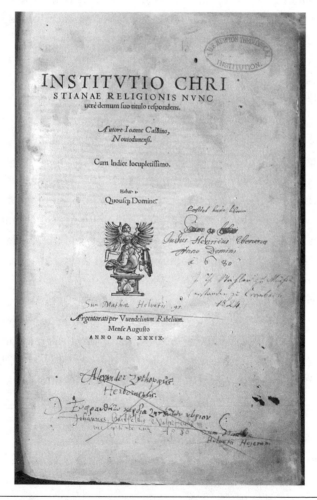

Figure 5.1. Title page of the 1539 edition of the *Institutes*. Courtesy of the H. Henry Meeter Center

The most notable addition was new material that became the first two chapters. In these, Calvin expands his discussion of the knowledge of God and knowledge of self into two separate chapters. Whereas in the 1536 edition, he only dealt with the topics in a few short paragraphs in the first chapter of the book, in the new edition he wrote two rather long chapters. The first chapter focuses extensively on the knowledge of God, including a good amount of discussion on the way humans can know God through Scripture. In the second chapter, Calvin explains the meanings of the knowledge of self and free will. He then added separate chapters on repentance, justification, the similarities and differences between the Old and New Testaments, and predestination and providence. After discussing the sacraments in general, he wrote one chapter on baptism and another on the Lord's Supper. Toward the end of the book, he split the last chapter of the 1536 edition of the *Institutes* into four chapters: Christian freedom, the power of the church, civil government, and the Christian life.

An important change that we find in the second edition of the *Institutes* is the way Calvin discusses predestination and providence together in one chapter. He shows that God's providence includes God's saving work for his people. God is in control over all creation, and divine providence shows that God never departs from his work and his people. Even though human beings have fallen into sin, God saves fallen humanity through the saving grace of Jesus Christ. In his providential care for his people, God chooses the ones whom he saves. Therefore, in Calvin's mind, the doctrines of providence and salvation are closely linked. Salvation for God's people is secure in the hands of God who creates, provides for, and predestines them.

Subsequent Latin Editions of the *Institutes*

In 1543, Calvin published the third edition of the *Institutes*, which was then republished in 1545. Both were published in

Strasbourg by Wendelinum Rihelium. This version saw a further elaboration of Calvin's thoughts, with twenty-one chapters in total. He added one chapter on monastic vows and enlarged the discussion on the Apostles' Creed into four separate chapters. He also lengthened his theological explanation of the offices of the church.

Calvin published the fourth Latin edition of the *Institutes* in 1550. He reprinted the same edition in 1553 and again in 1554. They were all published in Geneva, the first edition by Johannes Gerard. The 1550 edition of the book is slightly larger than the previous version of the *Institutes*. He added a long explanation on the conscience, and he subdivided the chapters into numbered paragraphs so the readers could follow along more easily and find particular topics more quickly.

> The 1559 edition of the *Institutes* is regarded as the ultimate edition of the book. The 1560 French edition is not to be considered Calvin's final version of the book because it was a translation of the 1559 edition and not an expanded version.

The final and most extensive Latin version of the *Institutes* was published in 1559. This version will serve as the basis for my detailed discussion and reader's guide in the chapters that follow. By the time of this final edition, the *Institutes* had grown into four books with a total of eighty chapters. In the title of this edition, Calvin clearly mentions that he had increased the amount of material substantially. The expansion of the material, to a large extent, was due to the theological debates that Calvin had with various opponents. As the polemics with other people grew, the explanations that Calvin put into the book also got longer.

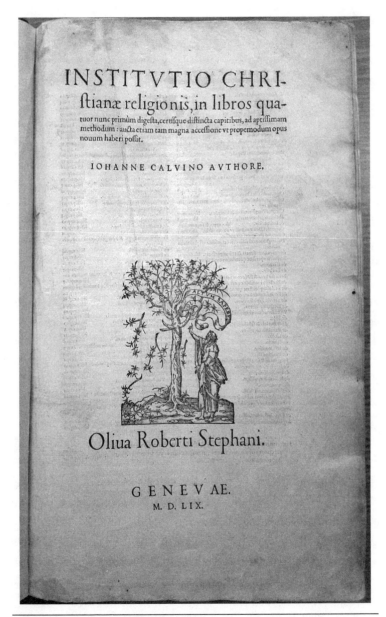

Figure 5.2. Title page of the 1559 edition of the *Institutes.*
Courtesy of the H. Henry Meeter Center

The French Editions of the *Institutes*

Calvin wrote the first edition of the *Institutes* with his fellow French citizens in mind. But interestingly, there was no French translation of the 1536 edition. Reports circulated that he had started translating the book into French but never completed it. The first French translation of the book was published in 1541, which was based on the 1539 Latin version of the *Institutes*. This translation was published shortly after he returned to Geneva. The French translation of the book benefited those who did not read Latin. Through this translation, Calvin was able to reach the people of France with his Christian beliefs. Sadly, though, because France was opposed to the spread of the Reformed movement, both the Latin and French version of the *Institutes* were banned in France, and anyone found owning a copy of the book would be reported to the authorities. In English today there are two modern translations of the 1541 French edition of the *Institutes*. One, translated by Elsie McKee, was published in 2009.[2] The other was translated by Robert White and was first published in 2014.[3]

A few years after the first French edition, the 1543 Latin edition of the *Institutes* was translated into French and was published in Geneva in 1545. The translation of the book into French was a complement to Calvin's insistence that Christians in Geneva should know the teaching of the Christian faith in their mother tongue. The book would help the people to understand the doctrines of the church more deeply as they heard the message of the Bible preached every Sunday in their language.

The fourth edition of the Latin version of the *Institutes* of 1550 was translated into French in 1551, followed by three reprints of the

---

[2]John Calvin, *Institutes of the Christian Religion, 1541 French Edition: The First English Translation*, trans. Elsie McKee (Grand Rapids, MI: Eerdmans, 2009).
[3]John Calvin, *Institutes of the Christian Religion: Calvin's Own "Essentials" Edition* (Edinburgh: Banner of Truth Trust, 2014).

same version in 1553, 1554, and 1557. All of them were published in Geneva. These reprints showed that as Calvin's work was gaining more acceptance in Geneva, there was more interest and need for the people to read his theological thoughts in French. The rapid succession of reprints indicated that the demand for the *Institutes* in French rose as Calvin gained stronger leadership in the Reformed church in the city.

Ultimately, the 1559 Latin edition of the *Institutes* was translated into French and published in 1560 in Geneva. Although earlier scholars questioned whether Calvin did his own translations, modern scholars agree that he indeed was the translator of the book. Although the 1560 French translation was the last version that Calvin worked on, I always tell my students that they should regard the 1559 Latin edition as the final edition of Calvin's *Institutes.*

Suggestions for Further Reading

Greef, Wulfert. *The Writings of John Calvin: An Introduction.* Louisville, KY: Westminster John Knox, 2008.

Lane, Anthony N. S. *A Reader's Guide to Calvin's Institutes.* Grand Rapids, MI: Baker Academic, 2009.

McKim, Donald K., ed. *The Cambridge Companion to John Calvin.* New York: Cambridge University Press, 2004.

Zachman, Randall. *John Calvin as Teacher, Pastor, and Theologian: The Shape of His Writings and Thoughts.* Grand Rapids, MI: Baker Academic, 2006.

- 6 -

Book One of the *Institutes*

Over the course of the following chapters, I will carefully guide readers through the four books (or parts) of the 1559 edition of Calvin's *Institutes of the Christian Religion.* As we make our way through the theological topics discussed by Calvin, I hope that whether or not you agree with him on every point, you will be able to follow his logic and increase your understanding of the Christian faith broadly as well as the Reformed tradition more specifically.

In Book One of the *Institutes*, Calvin talks about the knowledge of God the Creator. Knowledge of God the Creator is closely connected to the knowledge of self. If we want to know ourselves, we must know God our Creator, and the more deeply we know God, the more we know ourselves as God's good creation. Here Calvin discusses what it means to believe in God the Trinity, the Scripture as God's way of revealing himself in his words, the creation of the universe, human beings as God's image bearers, and the way God cares for the world.

Knowledge of God and Knowledge of Self

Just as he wrote in all previous editions of the *Institutes,* Calvin opens the 1559 *Institutes* with an important claim, saying that all true and certain wisdom consists of two parts: the knowledge of God and the knowledge of ourselves. Right from the start, he joins two important elements of human lives—wisdom and knowledge—in an effort to show how we might know who God is. He writes, "Nearly all wisdom we possess, that is to say, true and sound wisdom, consists of two parts: the knowledge of God and of ourselves."[1]

FUN FACT

When you cite from the *Institutes,* reference it using the numbers that correspond to the book, chapter, and paragraph, not the page number of the edition you use. This way, your readers will always find the exact reference no matter what language or print edition they use.

In Calvin's time, educated people employed a certain approach to explaining their thoughts through a method called *scholasticism.* Within this method, people understood wisdom as knowledge of what is good and true, and therefore it was the ground for people to distinguish between true and false. For the scholastics, wisdom was one of the attributes of God. Knowledge, on the other hand, was understood as what people could acquire through demonstrations or explanations. Seen from this light, the scholastics thought that this type of knowledge could not be said to be in God, because God's knowledge was not something that he acquired. By connecting wisdom and knowledge as the primary foundation in doing theology, Calvin shows that Christian faith needs both components.

Calvin explains that we cannot understand who we are without looking toward God. Thus, knowledge of God and knowledge of ourselves are closely connected, and it is impossible to say which one comes first and which one follows. Quoting Acts 17:28, Calvin states

---

[1]John Calvin, *Institutes of the Christian Religion* [1559], ed. John T. McNeill, trans. Ford Lewis Battles (Philadelphia: Westminster, 1960), I.1.1.

that because in God we all "live and move," we cannot avoid thinking about God while we think about ourselves. Our very existence depends on God. And seeing that our entire life is a gift from God, he emphasizes the fact that every good thing that we have we receive from God. God created us good, but the sinful nature of human beings, caused by the fall of Adam and Eve, our first parents, brought us to our current condition, which is full of troubles and sorrows. Knowledge of our sinfulness leads us into humility, because when we look up toward God, we know that we are in need. Furthermore, he argues that we cannot seek God earnestly unless we fully understand that in ourselves we only find misery and despair. But if we humbly recognize our miserable condition because of our sin, we will be able to seek God, and led by his hand, we can find him.

The topic of knowledge of God and knowledge of self runs through the entire *Institutes*. Calvin builds on this foundational idea to expand his theological view. Starting with the knowledge of God the Creator, he shows that the universe starts with God's creation. When we look to ourselves, we learn how lowly and insignificant we are compared to God. But as our Creator, God loves us deeply. The knowledge of God the Creator is inseparable from the knowledge of God the Redeemer. Here Calvin points to the eternal and unchanging nature of God, who is the Trinity. Creation and redemption are not separable because the God who creates is also the God who redeems. As we will see in the following chapters of this book, redemption is the work of the triune God. The knowledge of God the Creator and Redeemer gives us the understanding that our God is an unchanging God and therefore, when human beings fall into sin, redemption is readily available. So when we look at ourselves, we find that as God's creation we were originally good because God is good. We fell into sin by our own choice. God the Redeemer gives us the redemption made possible by Christ, the second person of the Trinity. We receive this redemption by the power of the Holy Spirit, who unites us with Christ. The following chart will help you visualize how knowledge of God and knowledge of ourselves are interconnected in Calvin's theology.

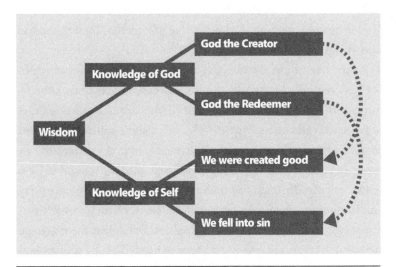

Figure 6.1. Knowledge of God and knowledge of self

In the *Institutes*, Calvin clearly shows the reality of sin as corruption of everything that is in us. He keeps contrasting the perfection and goodness of God with the wretched condition humans are in because of sin. Retelling several biblical passages that show the awesomeness of God—and the sense of wonder of biblical characters such as Abraham, Moses, Elijah, and many others when they encounter God—he says that when human beings properly grasp the knowledge of God, they come to a proper knowledge of themselves.

Knowledge of God is not just about acknowledging the existence of God. It requires a deep, intimate, personal relationship with him.[2] This knowledge will lead us into a life of fully glorifying God forever. Knowing God should also mean believing in him and worshiping

---

[2]Calvin, *Institutes* I.2.1.

him. This true knowledge of God would have remained in human beings had Adam not sinned. However, even after humans fall into sin, God restores this knowledge through Christ's coming into the world to do the work of redemption. Therefore, the knowledge of God is twofold, namely, the knowledge of God the Creator and the knowledge of God the Redeemer.

As the Creator of the heavens and the earth, God also provides for his creation through his boundless power, providing the creation with every goodness that it needs to continue existing. This is what we call the providence of God. Calvin paints a beautiful picture of how God's providence permeates every aspect of creation. In turn, as human beings we are expected to respond to God with gratitude. Through this understanding, we are led to have piety, the fountainhead of true religion.[3] Calvin sees piety, which proceeds from the knowledge of the goodness of God, as the marriage between reverence for God and love of God. To fully understand and experience all his goodness, people must realize that they owe everything to God, that they receive full protection from God's fatherly love, and that they receive all blessings from God, so they can submit themselves voluntarily to God. Only when people know that their entire happiness lies in the hands of God can they truly surrender themselves to his complete control.

But how do we know this? The knowledge of God, Calvin explains, is naturally implanted in the mind of every human being. Because humans are created in the image of God, we already have natural instincts regarding the existence of God. To prove his view, Calvin invites his readers to look at any tribe anywhere in the world. No matter how isolated from other civilizations they are, these tribes always have some kind of religious system that acknowledges belief in a higher being. Even idol worship serves as a proof of this

---

[3]Calvin, *Institutes* I.2.4.

sense of the divine that all people have in their minds. Calvin calls this awareness "the seed of religion."[4]

According to Calvin, atheists suppress the sense of the divine that they have in their minds, and therefore they reject any belief in the existence of God. Calvin uses Psalm 14:1, "Fools say in their hearts, 'There is no God,'" as a way to explain the mindset of atheists. He says that such people recklessly throw away all thoughts about God, even though the knowledge of God already exists in their hearts.[5] Likewise, Calvin says that idol worshipers are people with confused states of mind because they want to worship some power outside of themselves, but they disregard the true God whom they should worship.

Calvin also criticizes those who worship God out of fear of divine judgment and not out of reverence for his divine majesty. To avoid God's punishment, these people turn to religious ceremonies so that they appear to be worshiping God while in fact they do the opposite, an act of hypocrisy. In expressing this view, Calvin seems to be exposing the mistakes of the Church of Rome, which he considers superstitious. In his eyes, all the rituals in the church that the Papacy created are not true acts of worship. Without actually saying so, he charges the Roman Catholic Church as a false religion.

Knowledge of God the Creator

If we know God in part by looking at ourselves, then we also come to know something of God through his creation. Calvin rejoices in the beauty of God's creation. He considers creation the mirror for God's magnificence and often calls creation the "theater of God's glory."[6] As a result, people can never miss seeing the work of

---

[4]Calvin, *Institutes* I.3.1.
[5]Calvin, *Institutes* I.4.2.
[6]Calvin, *Institutes* I.5.8.

God when they look at the world around them. He points out that the book of Psalms is filled with many praises to the goodness and beauty of God's creation. Even the smallest part of creation displays his beauty. All creation reflects God's splendor similarly to how a mirror reflects our figures, and we can see it wherever we look. He writes,

> Wherever you cast your eyes, there is no spot in the universe wherein you cannot discern at least some sparks of his glory. You cannot in one glance survey this most vast and beautiful system of the universe, in its wide expanse, without being completely overwhelmed by the boundless force of its brightness.[7]

The sad truth that Calvin shows us is that in the midst of the grandeur of God's creation, people fail to see God the Creator. Because of their sinfulness, people look only at the created order and therefore fail to see the Creator behind the wonders of creation. Even people in Calvin's time held ideas that in our time would be labeled materialist: the universe exists by chance and is not the work of the great Creator. Criticizing this belief, Calvin says that such people miss the most important knowledge, namely the knowledge of God the Creator. Many of these thinkers, Calvin continues, only focus on worldly and unworthy ideas about the universe.

Regardless of the brightness of God's glory in creation, when unaided by God's Word, we are unable to come to worship the true God. Even though there are small sparks in our minds that might direct us to think about God, they grow dim too quickly, and we are left to think about ourselves and not about God. Quoting Hebrews 11:3, Calvin reminds us that only true faith in God can lead

---

[7]Calvin, *Institutes* I.5.1.

us to understand that the universe came into being by God's commands. Therefore, it is also only through faith that we can understand the true knowledge about God the Creator and about creation itself. Then, reiterating the recorded speech of Paul in Acts 17, he adds that God has given all of us proofs and displays of his existence so that we do not need to go far in searching for him; God has shown his kindness to all humanity by giving us rain from heaven to water our fields, so that we have enough food. The sad truth is that despite all of the goodness of God, people still choose their own way, which is to ignore God completely and in so doing make terrible mistakes.

The absence of the natural ability in human hearts and minds to have a clear knowledge of God does not mean that humans have room for any excuse for not worshiping God. Following Paul (Rom 1:18-20), Calvin argues that humans cannot plead ignorance regarding the existence of God just because they are lazy and full of ingratitude. Calvin insists that God's presence is everywhere in the created universe. Therefore, none of our excuses for failing to acknowledge and worship the true God are acceptable.

Over against people of his time who believed that the universe was created instantaneously, Calvin insisted that God created the world in six days.[8] This view entails that creation unfolds one step at a time. The progression of each step is consistent with the power of God and God's overall work. Our faith, Calvin explains, should lead people to understand the process of creation and the climax of God's work on the seventh day and help us to welcome the quietness that the seventh day brings. In understanding the unfolding of the events of the creation, we are also guided to embrace the goodness of God our Father. Human beings were created on the sixth day, after God had completed all the other works of creation,

---

[8]Calvin, *Institutes* I.14.2.

so that they can enjoy the fullness of this goodness. Had human beings been created in the earlier days of creation, they would have had to live in a barren, dark, and unpleasant situation because they would have had no supply of food and other things needed to live.[9] This knowledge, Calvin argues, should bring people to be thankful to God and to worship only him because he is the Creator of heavens and earth. And this knowledge alone, according to Calvin, should prevent us from worshiping other gods.

> Calvin believes that God created the universe in six days to fight the incorrect view that creation happened instantaneously. The six days of creation demonstrates that there is a process and order in the way God fashions his creation. Believing that Moses was the author of Genesis, Calvin wrote: "Moses relates that God's work was completed not in a moment but in six days [Gen 2:2]. For by this circumstance we are drawn away from all fictions to the one God who distributed his work into six days that we might not find it irksome to occupy our whole life in contemplating it." (*Institutes*, I.14.2)

Perhaps surprisingly for readers today, Calvin spent a considerable amount of space discussing angels.[10] The book of Genesis does not explicitly talk about the creation of angels, but Calvin contends that they are God's creatures. Even though we read in the Bible that they serve God in a special way—Calvin calls them God's ministers—they are not equal to God. They serve God in order that God can shower his goodness upon us. Calvin dispels the views of people living in his time whose teachings about angels relied on

---

[9]Calvin, *Institutes* I.14.2.
[10]Calvin, *Institutes* I.14.3.

extrabiblical sources that elevated angels to a place just below God. Calvin's contention that angels are not any higher than other created beings would likely have given offense to these people.

Just like many Christian thinkers before him, Calvin believed that the devil was a fallen angel.[11] The Bible does not give us much explanation of how or when the fall in the angelic realm happened, and therefore Calvin only touches briefly on this subject. He writes that the fallen angels rebelled against God and became instruments of damnation for others. A prevailing view for many centuries was the notion that the devil holds enormous power. Some people thought that just as God has the infinite power of goodness, the devil holds the infinite power of evil. Calvin singles out Manichaeism, a false teaching that had existed since the time of Augustine in the fourth century, as holding such a view. He insists that this is an erroneous view because it takes away the power of God and makes the devil an equal counterpart of God standing on the opposite side of goodness. Calvin vehemently argues that as God's creature, the devil has only as much power as God allows him. The Bible calls the devil, or Satan, the adversary of God. This means that as we uphold the glory of God, we must fight and reject the devil and his works as much as we can. Because the devil is created by God, he does not earn his evil power from God's creation but from depravation. He brings on himself everything that is damnable.

Scripture as the Only Guide to the True Knowledge of God

While we can know something of God from creation, for humans to gain true knowledge of God, Scripture is our only aid. In Scripture, God tells us who he is so that we can have an intimate relationship with him. Calvin uses the analogy of the usefulness of a pair of glasses to illustrate how Scripture leads us into the knowledge of

---

[11]Calvin, *Institutes* I.14.13.

God. People who have problems seeing will be significantly helped when they wear the right kind of glasses.[12] In the same way, Scripture leads us into clearer knowledge of God. Calvin sees Scripture as God's greatest gift for us, because in Scripture God opens his mouth to instruct us, his church, so that we are not left without instruction. God does not just tell us of some kind of God that we must worship, but he declares that he is the only true God worthy of our reverence. The Bible tells us not just that God teaches us to be in awe of him but that he directs us to pay homage only to him.

God places us in the world to see his work in creation, and he also instructs us to have a close relationship to him and true knowledge of him through his words in Scripture. In the wider scope of theological reflection that stems from Calvin's thought, we call the way God tells us who he is the revelation of God. From what Calvin explains here, we can distinguish between the way we know God through the greatness and goodness of his creation and the way we know God through his words. In Christian theology, the first one is often called general revelation. It is God's revelation to us through his work in creation. It is called general, because all people all over the world can observe the world around them and see God's work. The second one is called special revelation. It is the special and specific way God reveals himself through his Word. More than general revelation can, special revelation guides us to God himself, to know him intimately, and more importantly to receive salvation or redemption from our sins through Jesus Christ.

The first step toward having the true knowledge of God is to accept God's testimony in Scripture with reverence. Calvin contrasts this with the actions of people who hold to false religions. These people easily forget God's revelation even though it has

---

[12]Calvin, *Institutes* I.6.1.

been clearly presented to their minds. But Scripture exists for
those who truly seek God, and it provides sound teaching to lead
them to God. Calvin believes that God gave us Scripture, his
special revelation, to direct us to know him after we see his great
work in creation—his general revelation. In Scripture, we read
about his character accurately and vividly. Scripture also tells us
God's actions from God's own point of view, not from our limited,
fallen standpoint.

God is the author of Scripture, and therefore it has authority
over all people. And we can only recognize the authority of
Scripture when we accept it as the words of God spoken from
heaven. Prophets and apostles, the human authors of Scripture,
never boasted that the words they spoke were their own. They testified that the words came from God. Calvin acknowledges that
there are people who challenge the Christian belief that the Bible is
the Word of God and that the human authors of Scripture were
divinely inspired. These people, he says, need the Holy Spirit to
convince them. The Holy Spirit, who spoke and inspired the human
authors of Scripture long ago, speaks in our hearts today to convince us that the words of Scripture are indeed the words of God.
Thus, the Holy Spirit is the only witness for the truthfulness of
Scripture. And therefore, those who are inwardly guided by the
Holy Spirit accept Scripture inwardly, taking Scripture's own evidence that it comes from the same Holy Spirit. Calvin writes,

> Those whom the Holy Spirit has inwardly taught truly rest upon
> Scripture, and that Scripture indeed is self-authenticated. . . .
> And the certainty it deserves with us, it attains by the testimony
> of the Spirit. For even if it wins reverence for itself by its own
> majesty, it seriously affects us only when it is sealed upon our
> hearts through the Spirit.[13]

---

[13]Calvin, *Institutes* I.7.5.

Calvin is convinced that the Holy Spirit's work in revealing the truth of Scripture is not to give us a foreign revelation or to start some new teaching so we can receive the teaching of the gospel. Instead, the Holy Spirit works in our hearts and minds to seal the teaching that God has given humanity all along. Therefore, when we read the Bible, we must be careful not to be led astray. Calvin reminds his readers that anybody who takes the true teaching of God's Word and implants any other type of teaching is to be suspected. He writes against the Libertines, who elevated their own ideas regarding God's revelation. Under the disguise that they had freedom given by the Holy Spirit, they exalted bodily pleasure. In rather striking language that reflects the seriousness of the issue for Calvin, he calls them the devil wearing the cloak of an angel.[14]

God the Trinity

Who is God? The Bible teaches that God is one, and the one God reveals himself as existing as three persons. Importantly, saying that God exists as three persons is not the same as believing in three Gods. In his explanation of this fundamental Christian belief, Calvin goes back to the very foundation of the doctrine that had been established by Christian theologians who lived long before him. The standard belief of the church regarding God is that he is a simple being. This means that in his very essence or nature, God is undivided. In himself, he is without parts, portions, or divisions. The Father is this one same God, as the Son is this one God, as also the Holy Spirit is this one God, yet the three persons are distinct. When the author of Hebrews calls the Son "the splendor of God's glory," Calvin explains it means that the very nature or essence of the Son is the same as the glory of the Father. Similarly, the Holy Spirit also shares the same glory. Following the teaching of the

---

[14]Calvin, *Institutes* I.9.2.

ancient Christian writers, Calvin states that God is one, single essence (*ousia* in Greek) who manifests himself in three persons (*hypostases*).

> The Christian doctrine of God as a simple being, or the simplicity of God, means that God is not to be divided into parts. This doctrine is fundamental in our understanding of the Trinity. The three persons are not parts of one God, because that would mean that the one, divine essence of God is divided into three parts. In the doctrine of the Trinity, the Christian faith affirms its belief in and worship of one undivided God who reveals himself in three persons. Each person of the Trinity shares all the fullness of the one divine nature, while each is distinct from the other two.

Calvin takes the time to lay out the history of how the doctrine of the Trinity developed over the centuries.[15] Most importantly, he explains the earliest controversy regarding the Trinity, which started in the early fourth century under the teaching of Arius. Arius believed that Jesus the Son of God was not equal to the Father in his eternity, and therefore the Son does not have the same essence as the Father. He insisted that there was a time when the Son did not exist. The teaching of Arius exploded at the time of the early church, leading Emperor Constantine to call a church meeting or council in the city of Nicaea in AD 325. Among many decisions made at Nicaea was the church's declaration we now call the Nicene Creed.[16] One important line in the creed is the statement

---

[15]Calvin, *Institutes* I.13.1-29.

[16]The version of the Nicene Creed that we read in churches today was actually finalized at the next church council in Constantinople in AD 381, when the articles regarding the Holy Spirit and the church were added. If you want to be precise in identifying the

that the Son is of the same substance (*homoousios*) as God the Father. The Nicene Creed had become the standard statement of belief of all churches by Calvin's lifetime. He reminds his readers that the church should avoid the mistakes of Arius and those who hold similar beliefs in their doctrine of the Trinity.

Besides grounding his theological teachings on the Bible, Calvin also listens closely to the voices of early Christian authors who lived long before him. For example, he follows Augustine, who said that the names for the three persons of the Trinity refer to the relationships of the persons to each other.[17] These names are not about the existence of three substances in God, because there is only one substance of God. So when we speak about the relationship between God the Father and Jesus Christ the Son, we can say that in himself, Christ is God, but in his relationship to the Father, he is the Son. Conversely, in himself the Father is God, but in relation to the Son, he is the Father.

Calvin explains the meaning of *person*, when we speak about the Trinity, as the synonym of *subsistence*, namely, a distinct special quality that is distinguishable from other persons but which shares in the same substance or essence.[18] The essence of God is the one who is God himself. The term *subsistence* or *person*, then, signifies the distinctions and relations that exist in the Trinity. According to the view of the theologians in Calvin's time, subsistence indicates a particular existence, or an individual instance of a certain essence. So in the Trinity, the subsistence (or person) of the Father is an individual instance of the essence of God, and the subsistences or persons of the Son and the Holy Spirit are also individual instances of the essence of God.

---

creed, you should call it the Niceano-Constantinopolitan Creed. But for brevity's sake, let's call it the Nicene Creed.

[17]Augustine, *On the Trinity* 5.6, in *Nicene and Post-Nicene Fathers*, Series 1, ed. Philip Schaff (1886–1889; repr. Grand Rapids, MI: Eerdmans, 1997), 3:89.

[18]Calvin, *Institutes* I.13.2.

Following the orthodox belief of the church, Calvin affirms the Son's full divinity and the Holy Spirit as sharing the same divine nature as God the Father. Following Scripture's identification of the Son as the Word or the Wisdom of God (Jn 1:1), he explains that the Word is the same as God's eternal Wisdom. By this Word, God speaks through the prophets and the apostles. Through this explanation, he shows his readers the unity of God the Trinity. When we understand God the Father as the one speaking, God the Son is the Word that the Father speaks, and at the same time he is also the Wisdom that comes from God himself. God then speaks his word through the prophets and the apostles. It is the Holy Spirit who inspires them to speak to the people on behalf of God. Therefore, the three persons of the Trinity all are together as one God in his work; in this case, it is the work of speaking to us through the prophecies and teachings of the prophets and the apostles.

Calvin further argues that creation also enables us to understand the Trinity in unity. Often, we focus on God the Father as the Creator of the universe, and we are right that he is. However, in Genesis 1, God creates through his word. On the first day God says, "Let there be light!" and there was light (Gen 1:3). Citing Hebrews, Calvin explains that the word that God speaks in creation is in fact the Son in action (Heb 1:2). And he interprets a passage in the book of Proverbs that says wisdom originates in God and presides over creation (Prov 8:22-24) to mean that it is the Son, the second person of the Trinity, who does the work in creation. He then links this passage with John 5:17 to show that just as much as God the Father always works, so Jesus does too. He emphasizes that since the foundation of the world, Jesus has always worked together with the Father. By showing that the Word has always existed since before the creation of the world, Calvin argues that the deity of Christ is affirmed in the Old Testament. The Trinity is always inseparable, both in being and in action. Creation is the work of all three persons of the Trinity, not just God the Father. And then, as God speaks to the people through the Holy Spirit, we can also see that the Holy Spirit speaks the Word to the people. That is why, together with John, we can say that the Word is God.

Calvin also appeals to the actions of the Son and the Holy Spirit to demonstrate that they are fully divine. The miracles that Christ performed when he was on earth are proofs that he is God, because as the Bible testifies, these miracles can only be done by the one who is God. The divinity of the Holy Spirit is also affirmed through his works. The Bible gives testimonies that the Holy Spirit is indeed God by showing us that he is the one sustaining all things and giving life in heaven and on earth, searching even the depths of God (1 Cor 2:10). Through the Holy Spirit, we can have communion with God. Furthermore, following Paul when he talks about the gifts of the Holy Spirit (1 Cor 12:1-14), Calvin states that if the Holy Spirit gives gifts according to his will, then he must be God himself. The Holy Spirit has the same divine power as God and indeed exists as God hypostatically, which means that the Holy Spirit, who is equal to the Father and the Son, is fully divine, just as much as the other two members of the Trinity are divine.

Distinguishing the three persons of the Trinity requires careful attention, as Calvin explains. While affirming the belief in one God, he says, we should not overlook that the unity of the Trinity also entails that each person is distinct from the other two. Quoting the church father Gregory of Nazianzus, Calvin says that he cannot think of the unity of God without being illuminated by the Trinity, and at the same time, he cannot distinguish the three persons without being carried up to the unity of God.[19] The names Father, Son, and Holy Spirit indicate distinction but not division. When we read in the Bible that Jesus prays to the Father, we understand that

---

[19]Calvin, *Institutes* I.13.17.

the Father and Jesus the Son are distinct from each other. Otherwise, it would be meaningless to say that the Son prays to the Father. And it was Jesus the Son who became incarnate in the world to do the work of redemption on behalf of fallen humanity. This means, for example, that God the Father did not die on the cross. Calvin affirms that the distinction between the Father and the Son did not begin when Jesus was incarnated but existed in eternity (Jn 1:18). This can only mean that the Son is equally eternal as the Father, and that the Son is distinct from the Father. Similarly, when Christ speaks of the Holy Spirit as "another," we can see that the Holy Spirit is distinct from him. That is why Jesus promises his disciples to send the Holy Spirit, the Comforter, to be with them (Jn 14:6, 16).

> According to Calvin, the distinctions between the Father, the Son, and the Holy Spirit in the unity of the Trinity are not in conflict with the simplicity of God. He explains that "the Son is one God with the Father because he shares with the Father one and the same Spirit; and that the Spirit is not something other than the Father and different from the Son, because he is the Spirit of the Father and the Son. For in each *hypostasis* the whole divine nature is understood, with this qualification—that to each belongs his own peculiar quality" (*Institutes*, I.13.19).

By rooting his discussion of the Trinity in Scripture while also engaging with the church's long-standing belief that God is one single essence who exists in three persons, Calvin seeks to explain one of the most fundamental—yet complex—beliefs of the Christian faith. By thinking of the Trinity this way, he encourages his readers to think of the unity of God all the time, while paying attention to the distinctions between each person.

Human Beings as Created in the Image of God

If God is the one, triune God, then who are we? Calvin believes that human beings are the pinnacle of God's creation. Humans are the best examples of God's justice, wisdom, and goodness. Circling back to the topics of knowledge of God and knowledge of ourselves, he shows that the knowledge of ourselves is twofold—the original condition when God created human beings, and the condition of human beings because of Adam's fall into sin.

God created humans with a body and soul. Calvin views the soul as the immortal and nobler component of human beings. In his theological view, he does not distinguish soul from spirit, while acknowledging that sometimes the Bible uses the two words differently. He clarifies that when the Bible uses the two terms together, they can have different meanings, but when they are used separately, they are synonymous to each other. He takes the examples of Christ on the cross as he commended his spirit to the Father (Lk 23:46) and Stephen's words before he died (Acts 7:59-60) to show that when the soul is released from the body, God becomes the eternal keeper of the soul or the spirit.

The spirit or soul is the seat of human intelligence. It is also the seat of God's image in humanity. Taking the biblical words *image* and *likeness* to function as synonyms for each other (Gen 1:26-27), Calvin reiterates that even though the proper location of God's image is in our soul, the entire human person radiates God's glory, including the body. To explain what the image of God in human beings is, Calvin directs readers to look to the restoration that Christ accomplishes in redemption. He says that we cannot understand what the image of God is by looking at our fallen condition. Sin has corrupted our entire nature, and therefore the image of God, even though not lost, is completely deformed. Christ, however, has restored in us the image of God that was broken by sin. He explains humanity's condition as follows:

There is no doubt that Adam, when he fell from his state, was by this defection alienated from God. Therefore, even though we grant that God's image was not totally annihilated and destroyed in him, yet it was so corrupted that whatever remains is frightful deformity. Consequently, the beginning of our recovery of salvation is in that restoration which we obtain through Christ who also is called the Second Adam for the reason that he restores us to true and complete integrity.[20]

Following Paul in Ephesians 4, Calvin points out that God through Christ renews our knowledge, pure righteousness, and holiness. From this he infers that in their original condition before the fall, human beings had these three qualities as the image of God in them. Knowledge, righteousness, and holiness are the excellence of human beings before the fall.

According to Calvin, the human soul consists of two parts: intellect and will. He describes that the intellect enables us to distinguish between good and evil. The function of the will, on the other hand, is to choose what the intellect says is good and to avoid what it says is evil. Therefore, the intellect functions as the guide for the soul, whereas will follows the intellect's direction. God gives the intellect to the soul so that we can distinguish good from evil and have the light of reason. The will exercises choice in a way that keeps our desires and appetites under control, yet reason keeps our will under control as well through the work of the intellect. Before human beings fell into sin, they had intellect, reason, will, and wisdom to enjoy the most beautiful relationship with God and with each other. Calvin thinks that Adam could have chosen to remain upright if he had so willed. However, the reality was that he chose to eat the fruit of the tree of the knowledge of good and evil (Gen 3), and thus Adam fell because of his own free choice. Adam made his

---

[20]Calvin, *Institutes* I.15.4.

own choice, and his decision brought humanity to its own destruction, which was only overcome by Christ's restoration of the divine image.

God's Providence

In the concluding section of Book One, Calvin turns to God's action in relation to the world. God never stopped working, even after he had completed the work of creation. God is the governor and preserver of the entire universe, which is what Calvin means by divine providence. Correspondingly, nothing that happens in the world escapes God's knowledge. For this reason, Calvin rejects all notions of fortune or chance. God's omnipotence means that God has the power to uphold the entire creation, and God's power is caring, effective, energetic, and always active.

In light of this affirmation of God's providence, Calvin argues, believers can have comfort in knowing that everything that happens in their lives is in God's hands. Believers can be assured that anything that could harm them is in God's control, including Satan. No danger can threaten believers unless God allows it to happen, and nothing can happen except by God's knowledge and will. Providence does not mean that God only works in a vague way, giving some kind of possibility for things to happen without God's specific action toward individuals.

As part of his discussion of providence, Calvin clearly opposes the concept of fate as unbiblical, and therefore against God's truth. The Stoics believed that fate is the endless chain of causes and effects in nature that happen without God's active work in nature. By contrast, Calvin affirms that God's providence entails that God maintains the heavens and the earth intimately, and the minds and wills of people are directed in such a way that they move how God has decided. Thus, nothing happens at random. Calvin agrees with Augustine who said that if anything is left to luck, then the world moves at random.[21] For that reason, Augustine excludes any happening that depends on human will, because things happen only because of God's will. Sometimes Augustine uses the term *permission* to show God's will, and for Calvin, this word should be understood in the context that God's will is the supreme and primary cause of everything that happens. Certainly, Augustine was not imagining God sitting idly in heaven, only allowing events to happen.

For Calvin, belief in God's providence provides total comfort to God's children. An affirmation of divine providence does not negate or deny the reality of evil. When our lives see their darkest hours, we can still believe that God is pure light, justice, wisdom, and love, and that he will always provide the right solution to our problems. Calvin points out that we frequently and foolishly measure God through our limited points of view. We are often too quick to judge God on things that we do not know or understand. In our troubles, we often complain to God even when we do not see the big picture the way God sees it. In this way, says Calvin, we have become arrogant, and we insult the hidden wisdom of God.

Responding to a common misconception about providence, Calvin argues that knowing about God's providence does not give us permission to live recklessly. Thinking that there is nothing we can do about life, some people say that there is no need to lead a healthy life, to avoid dangers when they are on a journey, or go to the doctor when they are sick. They argue that these are useless attempts to alter God's will. If God knows that we will die, they argue, what difference will it make for us to take some medicine to cure our illnesses? Consequently, these people also think that our prayers to God are meaningless. And with the same line of argument, these people also say that all crimes can be called virtues

---

[21]Calvin, *Institutes* I.16.8.

because they must be according to God's will. In his reply to such misguided arguments, Calvin explains that in their hearts people plan their courses, but the Lord determines their steps (Prov 16:9). In other words, God's eternal decision does not prevent us from providing for ourselves, arranging our own affairs under God's lordship and being responsible for our actions. God, who has provided boundaries for our lives, has also given us the responsibility to take care of it carefully. God gives us ways to safeguard our lives, and he also warns us about the dangers that can threaten us.

While Calvin clearly affirms that God in his providence is the primary cause of all that happens, he reminds us not to overlook secondary causes. These secondary causes are God's tools to bring us his divine goodness as he blesses us through the works of others. So, when we receive goodness because another person has helped us, we can see that God is the primary author of this goodness. But at the same time, the person who helps us as the secondary cause also deserves our gratitude. On the flip side of the coin, when something bad happens to us, the person who is responsible for the malady is to be blamed for the sinful action, not God.

Some people might find it distressing to emphasize God's agency, but Calvin views it as a source of comfort. Knowing God's providence liberates us not just from fear and anxiety but also from worries. Because nothing happens by chance but only according to God's perfect will, we know that we can confidently rest in God's hands. Our heavenly Father directs everything according to his will, and nothing can happen unless he ordains it. When we experience the attack of the devil, Calvin says, we should not panic, because we know that God is above all. Sometimes God uses the work of the ungodly to serve his purposes, but it does not mean that the ungodly will go unpunished. Calvin uses the relationship between Jesus and Judas as his way of explaining this biblical reality: Jesus had to die on the cross for our salvation. Judas was the one who betrayed Jesus. Judas's sinful action resulted in Christ's crucifixion, which brought about humanity's salvation, but that does not mean that Judas is free from his guilty act. He is still guilty of his own crime. In Book One of the *Institutes*, Calvin carefully explains what it means to know God the Creator. He discusses important doctrinal beliefs regarding God and how we can know him truthfully as taught in the Bible, which he regards as the foundation of faith. The knowledge of God brings us to the knowledge of ourselves as created by God but fallen into sin. In Book Two, Calvin turns to the question of how fallen humanity is redeemed by God.

Suggestions for Further Reading

Adhinarta, Yuzo. *The Doctrine of the Holy Spirit in the Major Reformed Confessions and Catechisms of the Sixteenth and Seventeenth Centuries*. Carlisle: Langham Monographs, 2021.

Earnshaw, Rebekah. *Creator and Creation According to Calvin on Genesis*. Göttingen: Vandenhoeck & Ruprecht, 2020.

Holder, R. Ward. *John Calvin and the Grounding of Interpretation: Calvin's First Commentaries*. Leiden: Brill, 2006.

Pitkin, Barbara. *What Pure Eye Could See: Calvin's Doctrine of Faith in Its Exegetical Context*. New York: Oxford University Press, 1999.

Schreiner, Susan E. *The Theater of His Glory: Nature and Natural Order in the Thought of John Calvin*. Grand Rapids, MI: Baker Books, 1995.

Book Two of the *Institutes*

In Book Two of the 1559 edition of *Institutes of the Christian Religion*, Calvin expands his view on the second part of the knowledge of God, namely the knowledge of God the Redeemer. In Book One, he had started with the knowledge of God the Creator. Having explained who God the Creator is, he then continues by showing that the God who is the Creator of heaven and earth is the same God who redeems humanity from sin. And to know God the Redeemer, we must know the fallenness or sinfulness of humanity that caused us to need a Redeemer.

Humanity's Fall into Sin

In Book One of the *Institutes*, Calvin had explained how human beings are created in God's image. In their original condition, humans had true knowledge of God, righteousness, and holiness. In Book Two, Calvin explains that because of Adam and Eve's sin, all of humanity has fallen into sin. Knowledge of ourselves therefore includes the knowledge of how we were created good in the image of God and the knowledge that we have fallen into sin. Without that knowledge, we would look at ourselves too highly and be blinded by self-love, that is, we might forget that we are sinners. Knowledge of ourselves in our sinfulness will bring us to the right knowledge of God, who is our Creator and our Redeemer.

Some people in Calvin's time misinterpreted the story of Adam's fall into sin as the sin of gluttony, as though Adam's sin was his inability to resist the temptation to eat the fruit of the tree of the knowledge of good and evil.[1] Calvin disagrees with this widely held view. He insists that the sin of Adam was a serious act of disobeying God. The very name of the tree, according to him, tells us clearly that human beings should have felt satisfied with what God had given them. But the tree was in the garden, he argues, to test how Adam exercised his faith. Adam's failure to completely obey God started with his pride. Following Augustine, Calvin explains that pride is the origin of all sin.[2] In his pride, Adam was not willing to subject himself to the authority of God. His action of eating the fruit signaled that he wanted to be raised higher than his status as a human being who was created by God. Instead, Adam wanted to be like God, knowing good and evil.

Following the account of humanity's fall into sin (Gen 3), Calvin emphasizes the disobedience of human beings as at the center of the fall. Adam forgot that he had been created in the image of God. His action demonstrated that he wanted to be autonomous from his Creator. Calvin views sin not just as apostasy but more than that, as a despicable reproach and offense against God. Adam rebelled against God because he yielded to Satan's temptation. In so doing, he put off the glory of God that had been bestowed to him in his original condition.

Adam's spiritual life was fully dependent on his union with God the Creator. Sin separated Adam from God, and therefore sin brought death to his soul. Calvin interprets this to mean that Adam imputed, or passed down, his sin to all his descendants, namely all people all over the world. Building his theological explanation on Paul's letter to the Romans, he states that all creatures are groaning

---

[1] Calvin, *Institutes* II.1.4
[2] Calvin, *Institutes* II.1.4.

and subject to the corruption of sin (Rom 8:20). Calvin concludes that sin and its curse affect all people, starting with Adam's guilt. It is important for us to see here that Calvin joins guilt and corruption to show the depths, complexity, and reality of sin. Yes, Adam was certainly guilty when he disobeyed God. But sin is not just about being guilty. It also brings corruption to the human soul, and that is why the sin of Adam was passed down to all the generations after him.

Early Christian thinkers called the inherited corruption that Adam passed to all his descendants original sin. Sin is the depravation of human nature that was at first created by God as good and pure, and therefore, it is not just about being guilty. Adam's act of disobeying God was a guilt that he took upon himself. But then, Adam infected his descendants with corruption because of his fall. Calvin explains that Adam stood before God not just as the very first human being God made, but he also represented all humanity because he was the root of all human nature. Therefore, in Adam's corruption, all human beings are also corrupted. This is what Paul meant when he said that through one man—Adam—all people have sinned (Rom 5:12).

Appealing to an important event in church history, Calvin disagrees with Pelagius, a Christian who lived at the end of the fourth and early fifth centuries, who taught that sin was transmitted from one person to another—or from one generation to another—only by imitation, not because of propagation.[3] Pelagius's theological error has a significant consequence for the work of redemption that Christ achieved. If Pelagius was right, and we sin because we imitate the sins of our parents, Calvin states, then Christ's redemption must also be understood only as an example of what true righteousness looks like. Instead, Calvin argues that Christ's righteousness is

---

[3]Calvin, *Institutes* II.1.5.

communicated to us inwardly. The redemption from Christ undoes the power of sin that has corrupted our entire nature.

Calvin defines original sin as a "hereditary depravity and corruption of our nature, diffused into all parts of the soul, which first makes us liable to God's wrath, then also brings forth in us those works which Scripture calls 'works of the flesh.'"[4] As this definition indicates, Calvin believes that the corruption of original sin affects all parts of the soul. Therefore, we stand before God as people who are justly condemned. God only accepts those who are righteous, innocent, and pure, but original sin has caused all of us to be the exact opposite of what God wants us to be. All people, then, are worthy of God's punishment, for all of us have sinned (Rom 5:12). The teaching of original sin also means that infants carry in them the condemnation of sin. Even when they are in their mothers' wombs, infants are guilty (Ps 51:5). Calvin explains that even though infants are unable to perform acts that are sinful, they already have the seed of sin in them.

The doctrine of original sin tells us that all human nature is empty of all the goodness that God created in us. In addition, our souls have become fertile ground for evil to grow. Since the time of Augustine, it had been common for people to use the word *concupiscence* to refer to original sin.[5] When he used this term for sin, Augustine referred to all the power of sin that affects our bodies so that whatever we do, it is all sinful. Calvin accepts the use of this word, as long as it refers to the defilement of whatever is in us, namely our intelligence, will, soul, and body. In other words, sin affects all aspects of our nature and being.

Sin does not just affect our physical bodies and our natural appetites. It takes over our minds too, as pride goes deep into our hearts. Therefore, Calvin disagrees with the view that sin has only

---

[4]Calvin, *Institutes* II.1.8.
[5]Calvin, *Institutes* II.1.8.

touched the impulses of our senses. Nor does he think that sin only affects our sensuality. He vehemently argues that the corruption of sin exists not just in one part of our being, but it is in all parts of our soul. He keeps reminding his readers that this sinfulness was not God's original design for us. Rather, we fell into this condition, so we are not to blame God for our present condition. He illustrates sin as a hydra with its tentacles lurking inside all of us.[6] The tentacles of original sin bind all descendants of Adam in the same fallen condition.

As he had discussed in Book One, Calvin believes that the human soul has two components: intelligence and will. Agreeing with Augustine, Calvin states that because of sin, humanity's will is no longer free to choose what is good. In sin, we can only choose what is evil. Because of our fallen condition, humanity's free will has been enslaved, and it no longer has the power of discerning God's will and righteousness. Augustine believed that only when God's Spirit works on us can our wills be free again.[7] Calvin then explains how in sin we no longer choose what is good, namely our true relationship with God. Because of the power of sin, on its own our will cannot choose to come to God. Only when God comes to us—through the power of the Holy Spirit to bring us salvation through Christ—can we be free from the bondage of sin. By our own good work, we cannot deliver ourselves from sin.

Even though sin corrupts our entire nature, that does not mean that we are completely incapable of doing good acts as human beings. We can find people who excel in many good actions and humanitarian works. I am sure you have met people who are honest, selfless, and kind to others, whether they are Christians or not. Calvin attributes this goodness to a measure of God's grace that he gives to all humans. However, Calvin reminds us that we should not

---

[6]Calvin, *Institutes* II.3.2.
[7]Calvin, *Institutes* II.3.7.

confuse this grace with the saving grace of Jesus that cleanses us from our sins. The grace that Calvin discusses here, often called common grace by theologians after him, is a kind of grace that restrains sin in the hearts of people. Calvin illustrates this grace as a bridle on a horse. As the rider can control the horse using the bridle, so too God limits the perversity of our sinful nature.

Because our will is in bondage, we cannot even initiate a move toward goodness by coming to God for the repentance that will lead us to forgiveness. Calvin argues that according to Scripture, such a movement toward God can only happen when we receive the special grace of God. He explains that sin does not cause us to lose our will, but it causes us to lose the soundness of our will. Therefore, in our corrupt nature, we sin necessarily. This also means that we sin willingly. We are not compelled to sin, but we do so voluntarily. Sin comes out of our innermost being and by the inclination of our hearts, not because we are led by some power from the outside to sin.

What are we to do in this situation? Thankfully, Calvin reminds his readers, God gives us the remedy for our sin. His divine grace corrects and cures the corruption of our nature though Jesus Christ, who has come to undo the corruption of sin in our nature. Appealing to Scripture, Calvin argues that God is the origin of our conversion, not us (Phil 1:6). God begins his work in us first by awakening love and desires to find righteousness. God bends, forms, and directs our hearts toward righteousness. This is the regeneration of our soul, and it is the beginning of our spiritual life.

Importantly, Calvin completely excludes our participation in the effort to gain salvation. According to the Roman Catholic doctrine of salvation, humanity cooperates with God's grace to bring about our salvation. However, according to Calvin and most Protestant Reformers, the whole of salvation comes only from God. Even faith, Calvin says, is a free gift from God. We cannot generate our own faith. God actively works in us to bring us back to him, and the Spirit of God is the one governing and directing our hearts. And as the gift of regeneration is truly from God, perseverance, too, is God's free gift for us. This means that to continue to follow God and to persist in our faith are not our works. The first grace that God gives us, salvation through Christ, is followed by the second grace, the grace of perseverance.[8]

Calvin is adamant that redemption for fallen humanity is only found in Jesus Christ. The Redeemer is the Son of God who came into the world as a real human to be the only mediator between God and humanity. Because we have fallen from life into death, it will be useless just knowing who God is unless we are also given the saving faith that will bring us back to God. Just by observing our human nature or creation, we cannot come to the true knowledge of God the Creator, let alone the knowledge of God our Redeemer. But by the mercy and grace of God, we can have eternal life with him.

The Law of God

What is the role of the Old Testament in the Christian life? Calvin addresses this question by affirming that the entire Old Testament was a preparation for the coming of Christ the Redeemer. What Calvin refers to as "the Law" is the entire law that God handed down to Moses, not just the Ten Commandments but including the ceremonial laws and the sacrificial system of the Old Testament. Even though people in the Old Testament did not know Christ, Calvin argues, the law led them to see Christ from afar. Christ, therefore, functions like a double-sided mirror; he is reflected on both sides and through both testaments.[9]

The law contains moral law that renders all people inexcusable. It reflects the perfection and righteousness of God. People are

[8]Calvin, *Institutes* II.3.11.
[9]Calvin, *Institutes* II.7.2.

measured against this standard, and they are required to follow God's law and to keep it in their lives faithfully. However, due to sin, nobody can ever measure up to God's righteousness. None of us can observe the law of God without blemish. This means that we are under God's wrath and his just punishment for our inability to keep his law.

But does the law have a role in the Christian life, then? Calvin argues that the law has three functions for Christians. First, the law warns, informs, and convicts us of our sin, revealing to us that we are incapable of being righteous before God on our own. As he does in other parts of the *Institutes*, Calvin appeals to the metaphor of mirrors to illustrate his point. In this case, he uses a mirror to explain what the law does to us: just as we look at ourselves in the mirror and discover there are spots on our face, when we look into the law of God, we see our own weaknesses as well as our inability to be right before God (Rom 3:20). Calvin affirmed that the law shows us our iniquity and then drives us to come to God to search for his grace in Christ. Second, the law restrains people from committing crimes and other injuries against other people. People's fear of legal punishments will prevent them from harming others, and sometimes people refrain from doing evil not because they want to honor and glorify God but because they do not want to be put to shame for having been caught doing those bad actions. Calvin argues that this is what Paul meant when he said that the law was given not for the just but for the unjust, or for the unholy and the profane (1 Tim 1:9-10). Finally, the third use of the law is for believers whose hearts have been moved by the Holy Spirit.[10] For God's people, the law shows them his will, and it also leads them to live in righteousness. Therefore, for believers, the law is not a curse but a reminder to strive to follow God. You might say, then, that

---

[10]It is worth noting here that Luther did not accept the third use of the law, but other Reformers such as Melanchthon did.

according to Calvin, the law has both negative (revealing sin, retraining people) and positive (leading into holiness) roles.

The Ten Commandments

Among Old Testament texts, the Ten Commandments (Ex 20:1-17; Deut 5:6-21) have been a popular feature in Christian writing and encouragement for living a holy life. Indeed, Calvin included reflections on the Ten Commandments in his *Institutes* beginning with the first edition. Within the discussion of the law of God in Book Two, then, Calvin explains the meaning of the Ten Commandments. In keeping with his view of the positive role of the law in general, he believes that the commandments function as guidance for people to revere God and to worship him correctly. By keeping them, we learn how to conform our lives to God's will. Calvin is aware that the Ten Commandments contain promises and threats of punishments. These show us that God rewards people who are obedient to him, but at the same time God also punishes those who show contempt for his sovereignty. Outwardly, the Ten Commandments mold us to be devoted to God, and inwardly, they create spiritual righteousness in our hearts.

According to Calvin's reading of the text, the commandments and prohibitions in the Ten Commandments have meaning beyond the literal words. He interprets each commandment as a call to do something and to refrain from doing something. For example, the commandment to honor our father and mother means that we must also honor the other people whom God gives us as leaders. Also, when we read a command, we don't just follow it; we must also avoid the opposite.

The Ten Commandments are commonly divided into two tables. The first one focuses on our duties in reference to God, while the second is concerned with our call to love and care for our fellow human beings. Calvin calls the duty to worship God the beginning and foundation of our righteousness. Accordingly, in the first table of the law, God teaches us the proper duties of our faith. Through these duties, we worship God's majesty. The second table shows us that having revered God's name, we must conduct ourselves among and with others in ways that reflect our faith in God.

The first commandment, "I am the LORD your God, who brought you out of the land of Egypt, out of the house of slavery; you shall have no other gods before me" (Ex 20:2-3), lays down the covenantal relationship between God and his people. In God's covenant with Abraham and his descendants, God promises that he will be their God, and they will be his people. God has chosen his own people to belong to him, and he promises to bestow blessings upon them. In delivering Israel, the descendants of Abraham, from slavery in Egypt, God has shown his mercy and goodness to them, and he keeps his covenantal promise.

The strong bond of God's covenant with his people becomes the foundation for the prohibition to follow any other gods. This commandment calls us to worship only God as an act of total obedience.[11] The prohibition to worship other gods means that we should not transfer to any other being anything that belongs to God. Therefore, with the true knowledge of God, we contemplate, fear, and worship only him. Calvin reminds his readers that superstitious acts, even when they are supposedly done within the Christian religion, are equivalent to having other gods before the one true God.

The second commandment, "You shall not make for yourself an idol, whether in the form of anything that is in heaven above, or that is on the earth beneath, or that is in the water under the earth" (Ex 20:4), shows us what kind of God we worship. The purpose of this commandment, according to Calvin, is to show that true worship of God should not be tainted with superstitious rites.[12]

---

[11]Calvin, *Institutes* II.8.16.
[12]Calvin, *Institutes* II.8.17.

Without naming it openly, Calvin criticizes the Church of Rome for having been too superstitious in its ritualistic ceremonies, which he views as a form of idolatry. Then he explains that this commandment has two parts: the first is to prevent us from subjecting God under our own creations or representing God by a form that we create, and the second part is to forbid us to worship any image under the guise of religious activity.

The third commandment, "You shall not make wrongful use of the name of the LORD your God, for the LORD will not acquit anyone who misuses his name" (Ex 20:7), directs us to know that God wants us to uphold the glory of his name. Calvin posits three points regarding this commandment. First, our minds must think of God correctly, our tongues must praise God highly, and our actions must be directed to glorify his greatness. Second, we must be careful not to abuse God's Holy Word for our own gain or ambition. And third, we must not defame God and his works with words that go against him. Instead, we must speak praise of God's wisdom, righteousness, and goodness. Calvin sees this commandment as a direct parallel to the Lord's Prayer, in which we hallow God's name.[13]

Calvin discusses the meaning of taking an oath in connection to the third commandment. God forbids us, he says, from swearing using the names of other gods. Some people, he states, use the name of God in making false promises, and this action is prohibited under this commandment. Calvin reminds us that we demean God's name when we use it cheaply in needless oaths. However, he argues that there are times when making oaths is acceptable. As long as we take the oath truthfully in a necessary situation, and the oath is not taken based on our own greed or lustful desires, we are allowed to make an oath.[14]

---

[13]Calvin, *Institutes* II.8.22.
[14]Calvin, *Institutes* II.8.23.

The fourth commandment, "Remember the sabbath day, and keep it holy" (Ex 20:8), calls people to focus on and think about the kingdom of God. First, the commandment is God's way of giving Israel in the Old Testament a spiritual rest. In this rest people are called not to rely on their own work but instead to allow God to work for them. Second, this commandment also means that people should set aside a certain day for them to hear the law of God, to meditate on God's Word, and to be trained in piety. Third, the Sabbath also means an actual day of rest from work, so that people can have a break from their busy lives.[15]

For the church in his time, Calvin explains that Sunday should be the day of rest in keeping the fourth commandment, and it should be set aside for worship because it celebrates the day when Jesus was resurrected. The act of going to church on Sunday, which was enforced in Geneva, is not about keeping the church in line with the Jewish custom of Sabbath, nor does it have anything to do with the interpretation of the number seven as a significant number. Rather, it is about worshiping God on the day when we remember that Jesus has risen from the dead.

The fifth commandment, "Honor your father and your mother, so that your days may be long in the land that the LORD your God is giving you" (Ex 20:12), is God's way of guiding us through the people whom he gives to be over us, including parents. But this commandment extends far beyond our duty to honor our actual fathers and mothers. Calvin explains that in this commandment we are called to honor and obey in gratefulness those whom God has placed as leaders and guides in our lives. It follows that we are forbidden to take away these people's dignity either by contempt or ungratefulness. The practical application of this commandment is wide. Calvin indicates that God wants us to honor people who

---

[15]Calvin, *Institutes* II.8.28.

are our leaders or our superiors. He believes that people are placed in a leadership position because God has ordained them to hold that role. For that reason, we are called to treat them with respect.[16]

The sixth commandment, "You shall not murder" (Ex 20:13), shows us that God has bound all humanity as one. Each person ought to be concerned with the safety and wellbeing of others. Therefore, all acts of violence, injury, and harmful deeds are forbidden to us. Conversely, we have the responsibility to use any means at our disposal to save our neighbors' lives. This means we are responsible for maintaining peace and avoiding dangerous actions. There are two reasons for this commandment. First, Scripture tells us that we are all created in the image of God. For us to honor God, in whose image all human beings are created, we must regard the lives of all human beings as sacred. Second, because all human beings are united as one, we should also look at the lives of others as our own lives.[17] For this reason, Jesus taught us that if we have hatred in our hearts against our brothers and sisters, we are already guilty of murder (Mt 5:22).

The seventh commandment, "You shall not commit adultery" (Ex 20:14), teaches us that God loves modesty and purity. Therefore, all unethical behavior, in this case sexual immorality, must be put as far away as possible from our lives. Calvin reminds people to stay away from any filth and lustful intemperance of the flesh. God expressly forbids all acts of fornication. On the positive side, this commandment asks us to control and direct all parts of our body to do what is good. God has established the institution of marriage for us. We are to enjoy the union of marriage, and God sanctifies and blesses our marriages. Calvin sees marriage as a gift from God, and he disagrees with people who consider celibacy a higher calling, as

---

[16]Calvin, *Institutes* II.8.35.
[17]Calvin, *Institutes* II.8.39.

was common in the medieval church. At the same time, he also reminds people who are married that even they must not pollute their marriages with uncontrollable lust. Each husband must treat his wife respectfully, and each wife must also do the same to her husband.[18]

The eighth commandment, "You shall not steal" (Ex 20:15), teaches us to respect other people's belongings. On one hand, we are obviously forbidden to take away the possessions of others, but on the other hand, the additional implication of this commandment is that we should help others to protect their possessions.[19] God blesses all of us with the goods that we own. Stealing from others implies that we do not honor God, who has blessed them. This commandment also prohibits us from practicing deceit and dishonesty in our trades and teaches us to pay our debts. We must, therefore, make only honest and lawful gain. Our aim should be to help others to do well, and to let others keep what belongs to them as much as we can.

The ninth commandment, "You shall not bear false witness against your neighbor" (Ex 20:16), lines up perfectly with God's abhorrence of lies. Therefore, we must conduct our lives without deceit toward others. The commandment calls us not to harm others with words of slander or false charges. We are also forbidden to harm other people with falsehood through our evil words. The positive side of the commandment means that we are called to help others as much as possible with words that affirm the truth, so that we always protect the integrity of others.[20] This commandment is closely connected to the third commandment. We should not misuse the name of the Lord, as the third commandment tells us and here, we observe the ninth commandment by controlling our

[18]Calvin, *Institutes* II.8.44.
[19]Calvin, *Institutes* II.8.45.
[20]Calvin, *Institutes* II.8.48.

speech, speaking truth about others to maintain their good reputations, and spreading goodness to others.

The tenth commandment, "You shall not covet your neighbor's house; you shall not covet your neighbor's wife, or male or female slave, or ox, or donkey, or anything that belongs to your neighbor" (Ex 20:17), reflects God's will for us to be led by love. Therefore, we must throw away anything from our hearts that is contrary to love.[21] That is why our hearts must be free from any desire that causes our neighbors to lose what they have. On the positive side, this commandment teaches us to think only what is good and advantageous for our neighbors. Just as God wants our minds to be free from anger, hatred, adultery, robbery, and lying, he also wants us to stay away from the thoughts that will lead us into them.

Calvin's explanation of the Ten Commandments helps us to understand that the law of God is not intended to restrict us to looking at our lives with only the "dos and don'ts" of Christian morality. Many people have misunderstood Christianity in general, and the Ten Commandments in particular, to mean that being a Christian means living within the sets of rules that God has given, and therefore Christians are judged on how well they can keep God's commandments. When we read Calvin's explication of the Ten Commandments, we can see that according to him, the law liberates us from these constraints. Calvin shows, first, that we can keep the Ten Commandments only in a redemptive relationship in Christ. Keeping the law shows our expression of gratitude that we have been saved and that we live in the sanctified life that is guided by the Holy Spirit.[22] In this ongoing sanctification we live as God's children, and we joyfully keep the commandments.

---

[21]Calvin, *Institutes* II.8.49.

[22]We will discuss the topics of redemption, justification, and sanctification further in the next chapter.

Jesus Christ in Both the Old and the New Testaments

Who was Jesus? What did he accomplish for humanity? And how is Jesus Christ revealed to us?

In the Old Testament, God revealed to Israel that their sacrifices were meant to atone for their sins. Jesus is the fulfillment of all the ceremonies that God established for Israel. Calvin disagrees with people who made a sharp distinction between the Old Testament law and the New Testament gospel, as though the two reflect the work of two different gods. The law, as Calvin outlined earlier in Book Two, led people to Christ. People are unable to keep the law purely the way God wants them to do, and therefore the law brings them to the humility that they can never be right with God without God's help. Jesus is the only one who can fulfill the perfection of the law for us. Under the terms of the law, nobody can come to God through their own ability to keep it. However, this does not mean that once Jesus comes and the gospel gives us the good news of salvation in Jesus Christ, we can neglect the Old Testament law. We need to keep the law because it tells us what God wants us to do, and we need the gospel because in it we know that we are incapable of keeping God's law. However, by God's grace and love for us, he has given us Jesus to fulfill the demands of God's law on our behalf, and through Jesus' obedience to the law, we are made right with God.

Calvin takes Paul's teaching to heart when he says that the gospel is the power of God for the salvation of those who believe in Jesus, and that the Law and the Prophets of the Old Testament testified to the salvation that God had prepared in Jesus (Rom 1:16; 3:21-22). In this passage, Calvin points out, Paul was demonstrating that the promises God gave in the Old Testament had only one focus, namely Jesus Christ, who finally came to fulfill God's promise. Therefore, Calvin does not see the separation between the law and the gospel. The law and the gospel differ only in terms of their clarity of expression. Here Calvin differs from Luther, who maintained a greater distinction between the law and the gospel. For Luther, the law of God has demands that people must fulfill, whereas the gospel does not carry any demand. Calvin explained that in the Old Testament law, God made a covenant with the patriarchs of Israel to establish a close relationship with his people. This covenant is the same as the gospel's proclamation that Jesus has come to unite us back to God. In the Old Testament, God has given his people a close relationship with himself, and thus he has granted eternal life for them. The same principle happens in Jesus. God gives all the people whom he has redeemed eternal life in Christ.

Jesus Christ is God who became fully human to do the work of redemption for sinful humanity. Jesus came into the world so that human beings, separated from God because of sin, can have a relationship with God that is restored through his sacrifice. He writes,

> This will become even clearer if we call to mind that what the mediator was to accomplish was no common thing. His task was to restore us to God's grace as to make of the children of men, children of God; of the heirs of Gehenna, heirs of the Heavenly Kingdom. Who could have done this had not the self-same Son of God become the Son of man, and had not so taken what was ours as to impart what was his to us, and to make what was his by nature ours by grace?[23]

Christ is the only true mediator between God and us. In Adam, all people fell into sin and therefore they must be punished. However, no person can ever help themselves to be made right with God. Only God can save human beings from their sin. However, God does not need to pay anything because he is God. Therefore, Jesus, the Son of God, the second person of the Trinity, must

---

[23]Calvin, *Institutes* II.12.2.

become human to represent all people and to bear the punishment of their sin so that God's demand for justice can be satisfied. Jesus is God, who became incarnate with the sole purpose of bringing God's people back to him. Through Christ's redemption for us, we can become the children of God. In his humanity he has swallowed death so that we may have life in God.

Jesus is both fully God and fully human. This means that he has the fullness of the divine and human natures in his one person. Calvin explains that in Jesus, the Word became flesh (Jn 1:14); the two natures did not blend into something neither divine nor human. Following the orthodox teaching of the church that has been the standard doctrinal belief for centuries, Calvin states that in Jesus, the two natures keep their own characteristics unaltered, but the two are united in the one person. Each nature communicates its uniqueness to the other so that each knows the other fully and completely.[24] So, Jesus is both really God and at the same time a human being, but he is without sin.

Sinful human beings are condemned by God and dead in their sins. Salvation can only be attained through the work of Christ. Calvin reminds his readers of the words that Peter spoke in Acts 4:12, that there is no other name under heaven by which we can be saved. When we were still in sin, God was our enemy, and God's wrath demands that all his enemies be punished for their trespasses. God's wrath can only be expiated or appeased through the sacrifice of the one who is without sin. The death of Christ on the cross was the perfect sacrifice on behalf of human beings before God. Just as the blood of the lamb in the Old Testament atoned for the sins of Israel, the blood of Jesus, the lamb of God, washes away the sins of the world. By it God's wrath is satisfied. Jesus sacrificed himself so that he could be the ransom for many (Mt 20:28). The

---

[24]This doctrine had been established by the Council of Chalcedon in the year AD 451 and has been the standard of orthodoxy of the church ever since.

sacrifice that Christ made for us displays God's perfect love for us, because in Christ God is willing to redeem us from our sins. God's love toward fallen humanity preceded the sacrifice of Christ; God declared that redemption was to be made possible through the death and resurrection of Jesus Christ. Our sins caused us to be worthy of all the punishment from God that would have resulted in our condemnation in hell. But out of his mercy, God decreed that he would pardon our sins based on Christ's ultimate sacrifice for us. Our salvation is made possible only because of God's love for us. Calvin argues that we do not have any part in the redemptive work that Christ has done for our salvation.

Jesus' death on the cross displayed the great love of God for us. God used the cruelest form of punishment that the Roman Empire had in the time of the New Testament to show the most severe curse that Jesus had to undergo. On the cross, Jesus bore the curse of our sin. And by his death on the cross, he took our place in receiving the punishment God required because of our sins. The cross is also paradoxical. While on the one hand it shows the most severe form of punishment, which Jesus went through, it also displays Jesus' victory. By his death on the cross, Jesus defeated the eternal death that was supposed to be laid upon sinners. Through his death Jesus offered the most unblemished sacrifice. Ever since the time of the Old Testament, we read that blood was necessary to atone for sin (Rom 3:25). Just as in the Old Testament the blood of the lamb atoned for the sins of Israel, the blood of Christ washes away the sins of the people. Jesus suffered under Pontius Pilate. Here lies another paradox of Christ's redemptive work. He is the Creator of heaven and earth, but he was condemned under the power of a human being, Pilate, the governor of Judea, so that we can be delivered from the eternal wrath of God.

The Apostles' Creed clearly states that Jesus was crucified, died, and was buried. Calvin explains this credal statement to mean that

Jesus took our place for our redemption; the creed says, once again, that Jesus was our substitute. We were the ones who were supposed to be condemned to death. Christ allowed himself to be swallowed by the death that was meant to overtake us in our sinfulness, but he was not overcome by the depths of the abyss. Jesus allowed himself to experience death—not to be defeated by its power but to defeat it when it threatens to bring death upon us. Because Christ underwent death, we no longer fear death. This is the first fruit of Christ's death. The second fruit, according to Calvin, is that by our participation in the death of Christ, his death mortifies our sinful nature. Now we can be delivered from death's power. Christ's death kills our old self so that it does not have control over us any longer. Just as Paul has said that we are united with Christ in his death, we have died together with him to the world. Thus, Christ's death and burial function for us as double blessings: we are liberated from death as punishment for our sins, and we are freed from the mortification of our own sinful nature so that death and sin no longer have a grip on us.

Perhaps the most difficult article in the Apostles' Creed to understand is the belief that Jesus descended into hell. People in Calvin's time were wrestling with this statement, as thinkers before them also had. Some people interpreted the statement to mean that Jesus was buried in the grave, but Calvin disagrees with this simple answer. He said that if the statement were that simple, the creed would not have chosen such a complex concept. Even if that was the case, it would be a useless repetition because the previous line in the creed already states that Jesus died and was buried. Another common interpretation to the creed was that in his death Christ descended into the place where the people of the Old Testament who died under the law stayed waiting. Christ came to that place to free them from the prison in which they were confined for so long. The church in Calvin's time called this place limbo. Calvin does not think that this interpretation holds any value.

Calvin's interpretation of Christ's descent into hell takes a different approach. He does not consider hell to be a particular location. Rather, this statement shows what Jesus underwent on the cross. It was a spiritual agony where he experienced the severity of God's anger toward humans' sins. Christ's death was not just a physical death, because if that were the case, his death would not be effectual for our redemption. To appease God's wrath and to satisfy God's judgment, Jesus had to "grapple hand to hand with the armies of hell and the dread of everlasting death."[25] Jesus was put in the place of all sinners and evildoers, while he is God himself, pure and free from any sin. Therefore, Christ is said to have descended into hell to teach us that he suffered the anger that God has for the wicked people. Together with the previous statement of the creed, we can say that Christ's body was sacrificed as the payment for our redemption, and also that his soul paid a much greater and more excellent price in his suffering because he went through terrible torments as a condemned and forsaken sinner.

Christ's resurrection completes his triumph. Christ's death paid for our sins, but his resurrection causes us to be born again so that we can live in hope. By his death sin was taken away from us, and by his resurrection righteousness was restored in us. Calvin reminds his readers that they must always think about the death and resurrection of Christ together. One is never complete without the other. And more importantly, just as Paul has assured us in 1 Corinthians 15, Christ's resurrection guarantees our own resurrection. The death of Jesus was the same as the death of any human being on earth. And so his resurrection is also the same as the immortality that our human flesh will experience.

---

[25]Calvin, *Institutes* II.16.10.

Christ's ascension to heaven started his reign. In his explanation of Ephesians 4:10, Calvin says that Christ ascended to heaven to fill the whole universe. Therefore, even though physically Jesus is no longer on earth, he still fills all of us through his reign, which covers the entire universe. Jesus' ascension to heaven also provided a way for the Holy Spirit to come down. This was the promise that Jesus already gave to the disciples before he was crucified, that he would send the Comforter. The Holy Spirit has been poured out abundantly to all his people.

Jesus is now seated at the right hand of God the Father. This is an expression of the glory and the power that Christ has. God the Father is pleased with him. Therefore, the Father gives him everything that exists, and Jesus has complete control over all the universe. Now every creature in heaven and on earth should revere his majesty, glory, and power. This credal statement has some significant meanings for us. First, by Christ's ascension to heaven and act of sitting at the right hand of God, he has opened the door of heaven that Adam closed for us by his sinfulness. Second, Jesus, who sits at the right hand of God, has become our mediator, our advocate who intercedes on our behalf with God. We have a defender before God the Father. Through his intercessions, Jesus paves the way for sinners to come directly to God the Father. And third, we can see that the power of Christ has defeated the power of hell. Jesus has defeated Satan, and he gave gifts to all of us, namely the spiritual riches that God has in store for us. By sitting at the right hand of God, Jesus sanctifies us by his grace and gives the church, his body, various graces, preserving it from all harms.

Our faith in Christ enables us to wait for the day when he will come again to judge the living and the dead. On that day he will come back to earth again visibly, the same way he was seen ascending to heaven (Acts 1:11). Christ will come with limitless power, and all people will see him. This is a glorious day that we wait for.

His coming is comfort for all who revere him. For those of us who are with him, the judgment he brings is not one with destruction but with glory. As a prince who loves his people, Jesus will come to bring joy and peace. The judgment day is not like a tribunal when we will be put to shame because of our transgressions. Rather, it is the day when God brings eternal bliss, and God is the judge who confirms his promise of peace. The judge is our Redeemer, and we can rely completely on his goodness.

Because Christ is the only Redeemer for fallen humanity, and our redemption fully relies on him, we do not have anything to offer Christ for our salvation. We do not have any preceding merit that is worthy to be given to God for our redemption. The grace of Christ is imparted to us only by the merit of Christ. Just as Paul teaches in Romans, Calvin reemphasizes that the price of our redemption is the blood of Christ, and having received the righteousness of Christ, we may stand secure before God's judgment. The imputation of Christ's righteousness is without any work on our part. We do not fear punishment because Christ has substituted himself for our punishment. This word of comfort is what Scripture has told us. We can rely fully on God's love, mercy, and goodness without any worry.

Calvin's explanation of Christ as our only Savior gives us a complete look into the knowledge of God the Creator and the knowledge of God the Redeemer. In Book Two, Calvin demonstrates that the Redeemer, Jesus Christ, is the only mediator between God and fallen humanity. For him, the two sides of the knowledge of God mean that both creation and redemption are inseparable in what God does. The knowledge of God the Redeemer gives us comfort because salvation comes directly from God, and it does not depend on what we can do to earn it. In Christ we are saved without any merit that comes from us.

Suggestions for Further Reading

Hesselink, I. John. *Calvin's Concept of the Law*. Eugene, OR: Pickwick, 1992.

Moon, Byung-Ho. *Christ the Mediator of the Law: Calvin's Christological Understanding of the Law as the Rule of Living and Lifegiving*. Eugene, OR: Wipf & Stock, 2006.

Muller, Richard. *Christ and the Decree: Christology and Predestination in Reformed Theology from Calvin to Perkins*. Grand Rapids, MI: Baker Academic, 2008.

Zachman, Randall. *Image and Word in the Theology of John Calvin*. South Bend, IN: University of Notre Dame Press, 2009.

- 8 -

Book Three of the *Institutes*

In the second book of his *Institutes*, Calvin discusses in great detail the knowledge of God the Redeemer, in which he shows who Jesus is and what he does for our salvation. In Book Three, Calvin develops his thoughts by showing us how Christ redeems us. An important theological theme in Book Three, then, is how we are united with Christ. He opens this book by explaining that no matter how great Christ is and how much he has done for humanity's redemption, he is nothing to us if we remain outside of him. In other words, Calvin shows his readers that they are united with Christ and that they receive the blessings of Christ.

Faith and Our Salvation

Calvin believes that the blessings of salvation from God our Father can only come to us when Christ becomes ours and lives in us. Calvin bases this theological claim on several biblical passages, such as Ephesians 4:15 and Romans 8:29, which tell us that Christ is our head and that Christ is the first-born among many brothers and sisters. He clearly states that only after we become one with Christ can we possess all that he has. Faith, according to Calvin, is the instrument through which we can be united with Christ. Additionally, the work of uniting us with Christ is not ours. It is the secret work of the Holy Spirit. Calvin calls the Holy Spirit "the bond by which Christ effectively unites us to himself."[1]

Without the Holy Spirit, Christ is still remote from us, because we view Christ only from a distance. But when the Holy Spirit works to unite us with Christ, he becomes our head, and therefore we receive all the benefits of redemption that Christ has in store for us. In this way, we can say Christ is the firstborn of all the brothers and sisters whom he redeems. Calvin emphasizes the significance of the Holy Spirit's work by demonstrating that by the grace and the energy of the Holy Spirit, we become members of Christ. As our head, Christ is in charge of all our lives, and in turn, we can say that we possess Christ.

In this explanation, you can see that Calvin's theology is deeply trinitarian. He starts Book Three of the *Institutes* by showing that the blessing of redemption comes from God the Father. Jesus the Redeemer completes the work of redemption. And then the Holy Spirit attaches us to Christ so that we can reap all his goodness. The entire Godhead—the Father, Son, and Holy Spirit—works together for our redemption. I am sure you also notice here that, in Calvin's theology, we do not have any part in our own redemption; it is solely the work of the Holy Trinity. We are only the beneficiaries of God's goodness. I also hope you notice what he says regarding the work of the Holy Spirit for us. For Calvin, the Holy Spirit is so important that without him we will never be able to be united with Christ. I often hear Calvin's theology critiqued as not paying attention to the Holy Spirit. Or worse, people say Calvin does not have the Holy Spirit in his theology. But this is a mischaracterization of his theology of the Holy Spirit. Contrary to these misunderstandings, Calvin's theology places the Holy Spirit at the center of our redemption because without the work of the Holy Spirit, we

---

[1]John Calvin, *Institutes of the Christian Religion* [1559], ed. John T. McNeill, trans. Ford Lewis Battles (Philadelphia: Westminster, 1960), III.1.1.

are still foreigners to Christ. Because of the work of the Holy Spirit, which unites us with Christ so that we become the children of God the Father, Calvin calls the Holy Spirit the spirit of adoption. And because the Holy Spirit unites us with Christ, he calls the Holy Spirit our guarantee and seal.[2]

Our faith, according to Calvin, is the principal work of the Holy Spirit.[3] Our true knowledge of Christ the Redeemer consists of our receiving him. Citing Paul's teaching in Ephesians 4:20-21, Calvin explains that faith and the knowledge of Christ are inseparable. In this case, we can also state that faith is inseparable from God's Word, because our knowledge of Christ comes from God's own Word. At the same time, we must remember that faith does not just include knowledge that God exists. More than this, faith makes us understand God's will for us. In our union with Christ, we must know who Christ is, but more importantly, we must also know how he reveals himself to us. Faith, therefore, is the knowledge of God's will for us, which we know by way of God's Word.

Calvin defines faith as "a firm and certain knowledge of God's benevolence toward us, founded upon the truth of the freely given promise of Christ, both revealed to our minds and sealed upon our hearts through the Holy Spirit."[4] Clearly from this definition, faith is about knowledge. Particularly, faith is knowledge about God, all of God's goodness to us, and his will for us. We are saved from our sins because we know that God is our Father, and we know that God has reconciled us to himself through the work of Jesus Christ, his Son. Calvin clearly mentions that this knowledge is not just about feeling. This knowledge is certain and well-grounded on the work of Christ. Without the Holy Spirit, human beings can never attain this knowledge. In sin, human minds are darkened and

---

[2]Calvin, *Institutes* III.1.3.
[3]Calvin, *Institutes* III.1.4.
[4]Calvin, *Institutes* III.2.7.

human hearts are devoid of the conviction of God's will. But because of the work of the Holy Spirit, our minds receive illumination, and our hearts are strengthened so that we can understand God's goodness and promise for us.

It is now clear that according to Calvin, faith is real, and faith leads us into knowledge of God. Calvin is strongly opposed to the idea of implicit faith. In Calvin's time, the Church of Rome taught that people did not need to have an explicit faith to gain knowledge of God and his works. The Roman Catholic Church claimed that people, with their implicit faith—or something that Calvin calls blind faith—can come to God. According to the Roman Catholic Church, an implicit faith is an assent toward God without certain knowledge. By teaching such belief in implicit faith, the Church of Rome essentially sent a message to the people that they did not need to know the content of their Christian beliefs.[5] What the people needed was just an implicit faith in whatever the church taught. This teaching became a useful tool for the church to lead the people into believing anything the church instructed. This led the church to abuse its power, manifested, among other problematic ways, in selling letters of indulgence. Part of the reason why the church was able to convince people to buy letters of indulgence was because it taught about implicit faith. It was as though the church declared that the people did not need to know the biblical grounds for selling indulgences. What they needed was just this implicit faith, and as long as they did what the church said, they would get the blessings or the benefits of God's goodness. This implicit faith is willing to accept anything and everything that the church believes as true without robust knowledge of the objective content of that faith. Calvin's definition of faith as closely connected to the knowledge of God combats such teaching.

---

[5]Calvin, *Institutes* III.2.3.

Calvin's idea of knowledge as it relates to faith is not just understanding attained through the human senses. The true knowledge of faith requires that the human mind go out of and beyond itself to reach understanding. Because faith is sure and certain, faith can be strong and unchanging. Faith is not satisfied with a doubting and changing mind, therefore it cannot be happy with obscure and vague ideas. Realizing that unbelief exists in the hearts and minds of every single one of us, Calvin says that the Holy Spirit bears the testimony of the authority of God so that we can deal with the problem of unbelief. The Holy Spirit makes us really believe the promises of God for us.

Calvin criticizes the Church of Rome, which did not help the people in their uncertainty of God's forgiveness of them. The Roman Catholic Church, says Calvin, was confident that it understood God's great mercy as being available to everyone. However, the church was not able to ensure that God's mercy reached individuals, or more precisely, whether an ordinary person had access to God's mercy. Therefore, people's knowledge of the certainty of their salvation was close to nonexistent. What remained was constant doubt. Against Rome's misunderstanding, Calvin emphasizes that Scripture is full of the assurance of salvation. Faith gives us the assurance that God's goodness truly reaches us, and thus our hearts can enjoy the sweetness of this assurance.

A true believer is one who has the strong conviction that she is reconciled to God, her loving Father in heaven. Through this conviction the believer keeps looking up to God, trusts in his promises, and claims her salvation with firm confidence.[6] Calvin calls this a true experience in the salvation that God has prepared for his children. With this conviction, the believer knows for certain that she is an heir to God's kingdom.

---

[6]Calvin, *Institutes* III.2.6.

Having a firm knowledge of salvation from God does not mean that the believer is free from all anxiety or fear. Calvin clarifies that calling faith certain and sure does not suggest that assurance is never disturbed by doubt or anxiety. Rather, he says, doubt is a constant struggle believers face. The believer's conscience, in reality, does not always enjoy peace and quietness, totally free from troubles. What faith gives us, instead, is the sure hope that we have received God's mercy. He uses David as an example. David was a man after God's own heart, but in many of his writings we learn that his mind was often troubled. In the book of Psalms, David often expressed how much his soul was in trouble, up to the point that he condemned himself for his own unbelief (Ps 42:5).

Realizing that in this life we will never be totally free of distrust and that our faith is never fully perfect, Calvin teaches that we will always experience the conflicts between flesh and spirit. The believer always faces the tensions between the two. Spirit fills us with delight in God's goodness, whereas flesh fills us with grief because we know our sinfulness. But this does not mean that our faith is not sure and clear. Even when we are disturbed and confused by distrust, Calvin is certain that we are not thrown into the depth of the abyss, because in the end, faith will triumph over the difficulties that attack it. Even if we have the smallest faith in our hearts, we are able to see God's face. God is surely in heaven, but here on earth we can know him clearly enough that we are sure our knowledge is not just imaginary. When we have an intimate relationship with God, we become closer to him, and we have a clearer view of him too. Our minds, illumined with the knowledge of God, discover that ignorance gradually disappears. Calvin uses the imagery of a people shut in a prison.[7] If they get a glimpse of sunshine only through a small window in the prison cell, they can still know that

[7]Calvin, *Institutes* III.2.19.

the sun is out there, even when it is not directly visible from inside the cell. In a similar fashion, believers who still live in this world and are still limited by the physical body are already illumined by the light of God. This illumination proves God's love, and it makes them feel safe.

The Relationship Between Faith, Regeneration, and Repentance

Any discussion of faith must include a discussion of repentance and forgiveness of sins. Repentance is the product of faith. Sinners receive pardon for their sins from God when they repent. According to Calvin, repentance comes after faith. This is contrary to the view of some people in his time who taught that faith came after one repented from one's sins. Calvin openly criticizes people who hold this view.

In its Hebrew meaning, *repentance* carries the connotation of conversion, or turning again, whereas according to its Greek source, *repentance* means a change of mind and purpose. Calvin sees that the definitions from both biblical languages are appropriate because what really happens is that when we forsake ourselves and turn to God, we put off our old mind and put on our new one. Thus he defines repentance as "the true turning of our life to God, a turning that arises from a pure and earnest fear of him; and it consists in the mortification of our flesh and of the old man, and in the vivification of the Spirit."[8] Based on this definition, Calvin points out three aspects of repentance. First, in conversion, we turn our lives toward God. Second, repentance flows out of an earnest fear of God. Third, repentance consists of the mortification of the flesh and the vivification of the spirit. Mortification of the flesh means that we die to our old, sinful life, and vivification means that we live according to the guidance of the Spirit. Mortification and vivification come from our union with Christ.

---

[8]Calvin, *Institutes* III.3.5.

Repentance also means new birth or regeneration. The purpose of repentance is to restore in us the image of God that was broken or disfigured when Adam, our first parent, fell into sin. The new birth delivers God's children from the bondage of sin into the new life. New birth, however, does not mean that believers get complete freedom and that their lives are without temptation. The fight against temptation remains so that believers receive spiritual exercise. Through this exercise they understand their weaknesses. Even in the lives of born-again people, some measure of evil still exists, and wrong appetites still grow. Therefore, we need to practice fighting temptations constantly.

In regenerating his people, God destroys the power of sin by giving the Spirit so that they can surely win the battle. But even though sin no longer has power, it still remains. Even though, as Paul says, the old person has been crucified and the law of sin has been abolished in the children of God (Rom 6:6), some traces of sin still exist. Calvin believes that this remnant of sin exists to give us humility; we are always aware of our weaknesses. The good news is that God does not hold the remnants of sin against us. Rather, God ignores them as though they do not exist. We, on the other hand, know that only because of God's mercy are we not charged with guilt.

Faith and the Christian Life

What should the Christian life look like? Having explained how faith is connected to repentance and regeneration, Calvin continues with an explanation on how Christians should live. Once we know who Christ is and that through faith we are united with Christ, we must proceed with truly living as children of God. The knowledge we have regarding Christ and our redemption in him is doctrine. But doctrine, for Calvin, is not just a mere topic to be discussed, nor is it to be kept in a person's intellect. It must also reside within a person's heart and be lived and practiced every day.

While he thinks that perfect obedience to the gospel is to be desired, Calvin does not insist on perfection such that people who keep the teaching of the gospel less than perfectly cannot be called true Christians. It is true that people must be wholeheartedly obedient to God, but this does not mean perfection of Christian life at all times. He believes that God looks for integrity as the most important component of worshiping him. And this integrity is achievable through our singlemindedness in following God.

The spiritual life of a Christian starts when our inner feelings completely focus on God, as we cultivate a life of holiness and justice. Calvin perceives the life of a Christian as a journey. The progress in this journey happens every day. Success may be limited at times, but we should not despair so long as we keep our eyes on the goal of true goodness. When we reach success, we should not flatter ourselves. Calvin is confident that if we spend our entire lives seeking and following God, our journey will certainly reach the goal. This will happen when we pass from this life of flesh and are embraced in full fellowship with our God.

The entire life of a believer is a life of service to God. Service is not just something we say with our lips but a whole state of mind that is free from carnal desires and totally obeys the call of the Holy Spirit. So the first step in the journey is to give ourselves completely to God. The second step is to follow God's will and aim only to glorify him. Explaining what Scripture says regarding putting aside our selfish ambitions (Phil 2:3), Calvin says that Scripture does not just tell us to remove unnecessary desires for wealth, power, or popularity but rather teaches us to wipe out all ambition for worldly glory. We must discipline ourselves to think that all our life must deal with God only. This is the self-denial that Christ clearly emphasizes for his disciples (Mt 16:24).

Self-denial leads us to seek the good of our neighbors. In our sinful nature we are inclined to love ourselves. But Scripture clearly shows us that we are called to use our lives for the good of the whole church. Calvin takes Paul's teaching about the church as Christ's body (1 Cor 12:12) to mean that we express our self-denial and show love toward others because we are all members of the body of Christ. The church, therefore, is the avenue for us to show goodwill and kindness. We are empowered to be God's stewards in the context of the church. Here, we can put our neighbor's advantage above our own.

Love is the key for us to be able to deny ourselves. Calvin is convinced that God wants us to love and to do good for everyone, even when many people do not deserve our love. The reason for this is because people are created in the image of God. Here Calvin says that we are to love everyone regardless of their faith. But because in believers the image of God has been restored through redemption in Christ, Calvin goes a step further to give an even stronger reason to show more love toward fellow believers. Furthermore, in loving others and helping others selflessly, we must put ourselves in their place so that we can completely understand what they are going through. Similarly, we should not look down on those less fortunate than us.

The first part of self-denial is to bear our crosses (Mt 16:24). Calvin is convinced it is in our Father's will that we endure troubles and difficulties in life. Just as God the Father allows Jesus the Son to endure the cross, God also wants all his children to go through challenging situations in life. Calvin acknowledges the bitterness of the cross that Christians must bear. However, he also believes that the bitterness of the cross is made sweet when we realize that, the more greatly we suffer, the stronger our fellowship with Christ becomes. Christ was fully obedient to the Father when he died on the cross. When we are obedient to God in bearing our own cross, we perform an exercise of faith. Paul teaches that the challenges we undergo in life will produce patience, and patience produces character (Rom 5:3-4). Calvin believes patience gives believers experiential proof that God truly provides for his children as he has promised. At the same time, patience trains God's children to be obedient to him. Through obedience to God, we build our Christian character. The Lord uses our crosses to prevent us from being arrogant regarding our material wealth, from being proud when we receive honor, or from being boastful of our accomplishments. Each of us goes through different kinds of challenges in life, but all of us are formed in our Christian character through bearing our crosses.

The second part of self-denial is to meditate on our future life. While we live in this world, we go through all sorts of tribulations. Because God knows that we are naturally inclined to love everything this present world offers us, he allows us to go through hardship. God keeps reminding us through troubles that we should not cling too closely to worldly goods. Calvin uses concrete examples to explain what God gives us so that we are not preoccupied with this world. He says that God allows us to undergo war, disasters, or riots so that we do not rely on false hopes of deep, lasting peace. To keep us from becoming too ambitious about our own prosperity, God allows us to undergo failure that brings us to poverty. So that we are not preoccupied with married life, God gives us a difficult spouse or terrible children. We suffer from illnesses, and God can show us that human life is fleeting. These are actual examples of the crosses that we must bear. But when we look beyond these troubles, we see that our crown of life lies in heaven. We will never long for the future joy of heaven until we fully understand the temporary nature of all that we have in this world.

Scripture gives us ample teaching on how to live properly in this life so that we can enjoy earthly blessings. Calvin is not opposed to material possessions as long as they are used in moderation. In all reality, we need certain material goods to live. But he also reminds his readers that they must be careful in using their wealth. They must use their money to help others in need, according to the way they see fit. He thinks that a rigid law from the church to instruct how the congregation should use their money for charity is not beneficial. Each one of us should use our own conscience in determining the way we enjoy our prosperity.

The main principle in using our material possession is to understand that all that we have comes from God, and we should not abuse it. God intends it for our good and not for our destruction, and therefore we must keep this in mind at all times. God creates food for us to enjoy and not merely to nourish our bodies. Clothing is for us to create beauty and honor and not simply to cover our bodies. Herbs, fruits, and trees are filled with grace and perfume in and of themselves, just as much as they are beneficial for human consumption. Therefore we are to enjoy them to the fullest. In short, Calvin says that nature is full of wonderful qualities for us to find delight in, and we have every right to use them properly. We have the liberty to use them, but we are not to abuse them. Furthermore, he reminds us not to be excessive in using the goodness that God has given us. People often fall into the trap of overindulging in food, clothing, perfume, and other material objects. Christians should restrain from licentious abuse, as Paul reminds us in Romans 13:14.

The safest and easiest way to restrain ourselves from abusing God's gifts is by despising the present life and focusing our minds on the future life. Calvin gives us two simple rules. First, we make it our aim to use the world as if it barely existed, so that we cut off all that hinders us from eternal life. Second, we must learn to be patient and calm when we face poverty so that we exercise moderation when we have plenty. Calvin calls moderation a sign of significant progress in the school of Christ,[9] and he urges those who do not have great possessions to learn to deal with their limitation patiently. They should not feel ashamed for being poor, nor should they resent a simple meal. Without this kind of patience, such people would easily struggle with overindulgence, pride, and boasting as soon as they have the means to buy these material goods. He reminds us that God does not approve of such behavior.

Justification by Faith Alone

As we are united with Christ and we grasp him by faith, we receive double grace from God. First, when we are reconciled to God by the goodness and righteousness of Christ, no longer will God be a judge over our sinfulness but rather our loving and gracious Father. Second, sanctified by the Holy Spirit, we may live in blamelessness and purity.[10] In this part of the *Institutes* Calvin shows us the two sides of salvation or redemption, namely justification and sanctification. He sees justification as "the main hinge on which religion turns."[11] He says this because in his mind, without justification we do not have a foundation on which to establish our salvation, and therefore we will not be able to build piety toward God.

Justification. Calvin challenges the theological idea that we are justified by the good works that we produce. He teaches that people are justified before God's eyes when in God's judgment they are considered righteous, and God accepts them because of that righteousness. As long as they remain sinners, God will not justify them, because sin carries with it the wrath of God. On the other hand, people who are justified by God are no longer regarded as sinful because they have been acquitted by God and are therefore

[9]Calvin, *Institutes* III.10.5.
[10]Calvin, *Institutes* III.11.1.
[11]Calvin, *Institutes* III.11.1.

considered innocent. If we say that people are justified by good works, we must necessarily say that they have the purity and perfection on their own that makes them completely holy before God. In contrast, people who are justified by faith are considered righteous by God not because of the good work that they do but by the righteousness of Christ that is given to them. Calvin argues that no one can ever earn their own righteousness or holiness. Therefore, we can only be justified by faith. Simply put, justification by faith is the "acceptance with which God receives us into his favor as righteous."[12] Justification consists of two parts, namely forgiveness of sins and the imputation of Christ's righteousness. Justification is given to God's children once and for all.

Scripture clearly teaches that we are only justified by faith (Eph 2:8-9). Calvin provides an explanation on the order of our justification. First, God in his goodness lovingly embraces us in our wretched sinful condition. He knows that in sin we are completely without good works. Next, God influences sinners to be aware of his goodness, causing them to distrust their own works and throw themselves in the mercy of God to receive salvation. Calvin believes that faith causes sinners to be aware of their need for God's mercy. Finally, sinners will realize that even though the Holy Spirit has renewed their lives, they must not look to their own ability to earn salvation but only to the righteousness Christ has given them. Justification is said to be by faith alone because it is faith that receives and embraces the righteousness of Christ offered in the good news of the gospel.

Justification by faith also means reconciliation of the sinner with God. The Lord unites a person with him only after he changes that person's state from that of a sinner to that of a righteous person. God does this through the remission of the person's sins. Calvin

---

[12]Calvin, *Institutes* III.11.2.

argues that this remission is accomplished fully through the intervention of Christ's righteousness, so that we are justified before God. Therefore, we cannot claim that we have our own righteousness. We are justified only because the righteousness of Christ is imputed to us. Imputation means that Jesus Christ communicates his righteousness to us, and in a remarkable way, Jesus transfuses the power of his righteousness into us. Calvin builds his teaching on the imputation of Christ's righteousness on Paul's letter to the Romans, in which Paul says that through the obedience of one man, Jesus, many will be made righteous (Rom 5:19).

Justification by faith causes us to be humble at all times. No one can boast that they are justified by their own righteousness. Before the throne of God, no justified person is higher than any others. Therefore, in our walk with Christ, we must throw away all our arrogance and self-confidence. On the contrary, if we believe that we are justified by our own good works, we have reason to be boastful, and therefore we take away God's goodness in saving us from sins. But when we realize that we are empty before God, we in turn will be filled with God's blessings. We can only find confidence, comfort, and courage from God when we completely rely on and lay hold of the grace of God. In short, justification by faith alone leads us to give all glory only to God alone, and it also gives us peaceful rest in him.

Having discussed justification by faith alone, Calvin asks an important question about the goodness that we see in those who are not in Christ. It seems to us that there is an amount of goodness and justice demonstrated by people who do not have a saving relationship with Christ. There are people in the world, outside of Christ, who show virtue. Are these people not saved? Calvin turns to Augustine for an answer. Augustine once explained that all people who are outside of God, no matter how excellent they are, still deserve punishment because in their goodness they still contaminate the pure gifts of God.[13] Furthermore, Augustine explained that even though these people are God's instruments to preserve goodness in society by maintaining justice, order, leadership, friendship, and the like, they still carry out the goodness of God's work in the worst possible way. These people are kept from wrong not by love of goodness but by their own self-love. Calvin agrees with Augustine that these people are still not worthy of God. Although they may seem to do works that are good, their motives are still not true because they do not seek to serve God. The object of true righteousness, according to Calvin, is to serve God and God alone.

Sanctification. The other part of our salvation is sanctification. Calvin often referred to sanctification as repentance or regeneration. Calvin explains that the pardon of sin, an integral part of our justification and reconciliation with God, is closely linked to God's mercy. God leads us to live in obedience to him through the help of the Holy Spirit. It is the Holy Spirit who influences us to put to death the lust of our flesh. In the process of sanctification, our lives are consecrated to the Lord, and we aim to purify our lives as our hearts are disciplined to obey God's law. In this sanctification, our desire is only to obey his will and to glorify God forever.

Calvin is aware that even in our best efforts to follow God and to obey him, we often fail. He takes the idea from 1 Kings 8:46, "for there is no one who does not sin," to mean that even God's children, whom he has justified, still sin from time to time. And even the smallest sin is bad enough for us to be condemned by God. One sin is enough to wipe out all the good behaviors of an entire life. This is Calvin's way to prove that justification by works is just not possible. Here is where sanctification comes in. Our inability to keep our own goodness is remedied by the work of the Holy Spirit in our

---

[13]Calvin, *Institutes* III.14.3.

sanctification. Calvin believes that Christ does not justify us without making us holy as well. Justification and sanctification have an inseparable bond. Because Christ is not divided, once we are united with Christ, we receive his righteousness imputed on us. At the same time we are also made holy in him. Calvin explains what happens in our justification this way:

> The sinner, received into communion with Christ, is reconciled to God by his grace, while, cleansed by Christ's blood, he obtains forgiveness of sins, and clothed with Christ's righteousness as if it were his own, he stands confident before the heavenly judgment seat. After forgiveness of sins is set forth, the good works that now follow are appraised otherwise than on their own merit. For everything imperfect in them is covered by Christ's perfection.[14]

From the quote above we can see that, for Calvin, good works are important as we are sanctified by God through the Holy Spirit. Good works are not a condition or requirement for our justification; they are the natural outflow of the life that has been justified in the first place. Good works happen in the context of our sanctification. As we walk with God as his children, we seek to follow him and to do his will in obedience.

Once we are justified, we also live in freedom. Christian freedom, according to Calvin, consists of three parts. First, because we are not justified based on our ability to keep the law, our conscience must rise above the law. We still need the law of God because it teaches us to do good, but our obedience in keeping the law is not based on the thought that we are saved by keeping the law. Second, we keep the law not because we have to but because we joyfully want to. Third, in our freedom we know that we are not bound to

---

[14]Calvin, *Institutes* III.17.8.

observe the outward regulations of unimportant matters. This includes freedom regarding what we eat, what we wear, and observing certain holy days. He believes that observing religious traditions is right as long as it builds up our faith. But we should avoid performing religious ceremonies if we feel that we are under a moral obligation to do so. Here Calvin expresses criticism to the Church of Rome, which put too much emphasis on rituals and ceremonies that could become burdensome to the people and mislead them into thinking that those rituals are the most important act of worship.

Christian freedom is a spiritual matter. Its purpose is to give peace to the conscience. It is not to be used as an excuse for our lust or for abusing the material wealth that God has given us in this life. Calvin reminds us to beware of a materialism that brings us into a life of luxury with excessive enjoyment of food, clothing, housing, and other worldly pleasures. In moderation, he allows people to enjoy gold and silver, laughter, good food, and music. But he strongly cautions people not to fall into the overindulgence of these good gifts of God.

Prayer: The Chief Exercise of Faith

What role does prayer have in the Christian life? Should we even bother praying if God's will is perfectly fulfilled? Calvin places the discussion of prayer in Book Three of the *Institutes* right after the discussion on justification and sanctification, indicating that prayer is crucial for believers. It is the natural outflow of a life that has been justified and is going through the process of sanctification. As we walk in our journey to follow God in our sanctification, we must pray unceasingly (1 Thess 5:17). Because we are saved only by God's grace through the faith that is also God's gift to us, we need to have a constant relationship with God. We know that God is the gracious Father and that he has provided for us all the goodness we need, but if we do not pray, all of God's goodness will not help us at all. Paul speaks about the spirit of adoption by which we can call God "*Abba*, Father" (Rom 8:15). In our salvation we have been adopted to be the children of God. We can call God *Abba*, or father in Aramaic, the language that Jesus used when he was living on earth. A child who calls her father *Abba* has a close and warm relationship with him. When we pray, we can call God the Father *our* father because we are truly God's children. Prayer enables us to explore the depth of the riches that God our Father has prepared as treasure for us. Prayer digs up this treasure, and faith enables us to pray. Furthermore, our Father in heaven declares that our security lies in calling on his name. In prayer we can lay our burdens before God, and we can rest in the complete assurance that he knows all our problems. God is willing and able to provide for us in the best possible way.

We believe that God is all knowing, and God knows well what we need. So why do we even need to tell God what we need in prayer? Is prayer unnecessary? Calvin criticizes people who use this line of thinking to diminish the significance of prayer. He says that this argument completely ignores the reason Jesus taught us to pray. Prayer is not for God's sake but for our sake. God wants us to honor his name at all times, regularly acknowledging that everything in our lives comes only from him. This is the very reason we must pray. Calvin uses the example of Elijah in the Old Testament. When the prophet told Ahab that God would send rain, even in his confidence, Elijah still prayed (1 Kings 18:42-43). From this biblical story Calvin draws up some principles of prayer. First, we pray because we are confident in God's promise. In our prayers we tell God the longings of our hearts. Second, we do not need to be ashamed of our hearts' desires as we pour ourselves before God. Finally, we receive all blessings from God with deep gratitude as we remember in prayer that everything comes from God. When we get what we ask for, we are moved to desire God's favor even more.

Rules for true prayers. Calvin also gives us several rules of true prayer. First, we must set our hearts and minds in the correct mindset toward God.[15] When we pray, we must set aside our fleshly thoughts and worries that will distract our concentration in prayer. This does not mean that we should not have concerns when we pray, because we are told to bring these concerns before God in prayer. What Calvin means is that we must get rid of irrelevant worries that can potentially distract our minds when we pray. The second rule is that in prayer we only ask God things that God allows us to ask for.[16] Even though God tells us to pour out our hearts to him, this does not mean that we are allowed to request foolish and depraved desires. He criticizes people who bring silly requests to God that they are too embarrassed to mention to their friends. Within this rule Calvin reminds us that, in bringing our requests to God, we must be aware of what we really need. We must not pray to God half-heartedly for trivial matters. He also points out the mistake of the Roman Catholic Church in which people mutter prayers without thinking, with the idea that God will be pleased just because people seem to be praying to him. Therefore, in reiterating the significance of this rule, he says that every time we pray, we must be mindful of glorifying God's name. Hence, we must be completely mindful in every single request that we bring before God.

The third rule for true prayer is humility.[17] When we come to God, we must not be boastful or arrogant. Understanding that we have nothing to offer to God, we must set aside our self-confidence. Within this rule Calvin urges us to start our prayers with a sincere request for forgiveness and a true confession of our guilt. Closely

[15]Calvin, *Institutes* III.20.4.
[16]Calvin, *Institutes* III.20.6.
[17]Calvin, *Institutes* III.20.8.

connected to the third rule, to be humble, is the fourth one, to pray with real confidence that God hears our prayers. In this rule Calvin says that, driven by our needs, we come to God boldly because he hears our prayers and gives us what we need. In our distress God's goodness shines so that even our troubles are bearable, and we have hope that God will deliver us. Faith brings us the answer to our prayers.

An explanation of the Lord's Prayer. Like many Christians throughout the history of the church, Calvin considers the Lord's Prayer (Mt 6:9-13) to be the best model for our prayers. Jesus himself teaches us to pray this prayer, and therefore it is the best example we can follow. In the Lord's Prayer, Jesus teaches us to call God "our Father." This is an important truth to remember in our prayers, because through Christ we are called the children of God, and therefore we can rightly call God our Father. Jesus is the true Son of God the Father; Christ is the only mediator and intercessor between God and us. God the Father loves us in Christ, and he always accepts us with wide open arms, just as the father of the prodigal son in Jesus' parable receives his son who wandered away. God is not just a Father for us, but he is the most merciful and loving Father any of us could ever think of, however ungrateful we are, as the parable of the prodigal son depicts.

Calvin highlights the importance of the possessive pronoun in calling God "*our* Father." He explains that when we pray, we are united with God's children everywhere in the world—past, present, and future.[18] Even when we pray privately, we do not pray alone. We pray to God in the company of all believers who are the children of God. The Lord's Prayer teaches us that all God's children in community call him Father. All of us are equally redeemed by God and are equally made to be his children. All of us receive the same mercy

---

[18]Calvin, *Institutes* III.20.36.

and the same forgiveness. This bond of brotherhood among all of us also means that we are to assist each other and build each other up because we are all children of God. Therefore, our prayers must also reflect the togetherness of believers as one family in God. The prayer teaches us to focus on others when we pray, so that we do not become selfish in praying to God.

The Lord's Prayer, however, does not eliminate the fact that we also need to pray for ourselves, provided we always remember to pray for others as well. We must never forget the community of believers with whom we call God our Father. By this instruction, Calvin teaches that we must also pray for the needs of others as we bring our own petitions to God.

Calling God "our Father in heaven" means we acknowledge that God is far beyond any boundary, change, or corruption. Heaven in this case does not denote place or locality, as though God was limited by that place. Calvin believes that heaven is a superlative expression, meaning we understand God to be the most excellent of everything that exists. When we pray, calling God our Father in heaven, we are reminded that God is the ultimate ruler of all the universe, which includes both heaven and earth. God governs the world, and there is no other god equal to him. In teaching us this prayer, Christ tells us that we rest our faith only in him, and we are assured that God does not neglect our salvation. The eyes of God are always on his children and therefore, when we are in trouble, we have confidence in him who cares for us.

Calvin divides the Lord's Prayer into two parts. The first part is directed to God and has three petitions. The second part is directed to us and also has three petitions. The first petition of the first part, "hallowed be your name" (Mt 6:9), teaches us that we must revere God's name at all times because God's name is holy.[19] God must

---

[19]Calvin, *Institutes* III.20.41.

receive all the glory and honor due to his name. The opposite of this reverence is profanity. In this petition, we ask that God would vindicate his sacred name from all insults, and that God would compel all humanity to acknowledge his holiness. In this petition, we also give praise to God's justice and mercy. In all his works God has manifested his glory, and every day we see the glory of God in creation and in our redemption. This petition calls us to celebrate all the great works of God. This petition also implies that any impurity that obscures or covers God's glory should be eradicated, and all blasphemy to God, suppressed.

The second petition, "your kingdom come" (Mt 6:10), is closely connected to the first. This petition contains the same wish that the name of God be magnified.[20] Asking for God's kingdom to come brings us to deny ourselves, to devote ourselves to righteousness, and to aspire only to the things of heaven. God's kingdom consists of two parts: the correction of all the depraved lusts of the flesh and the willingness of our minds to obey his authority. So when we pray this petition, we ask God to destroy all the corruptions that destroy our tranquility and impair the purity of God's kingdom. The ultimate implication of this petition is that we must pray every day so that God may gather all churches from all corners of the world to himself, and destroy all false doctrines, so that God's kingdom may be established firmly. Applying this petition means we seek to withdraw from all corruptions that separate us from God, to increase our desire for the mortification of our flesh, and to train ourselves in the endurance of the cross.

The third petition, "your will be done, on earth as it is in heaven" (Mt 6:10), shows us that God is the king of the whole universe. We acknowledge that even though the devil and wicked people violently rise up against God, God is able to suppress them and can

---

[20]Calvin, *Institutes* III.20.42.

make them subservient to carry out his decree.[21] And thus we speak of the will of God in obedience as God's children, an obedience that is the opposite of the devil's rebellion. Heaven is joined with earth in this petition because in heaven the angels obey God and serve him joyfully. In the same way, we pray that on earth people will also serve God to bring everything under his authority, so that all rebellion and depravity are wiped away. In saying this petition, we drive away the lust of our flesh and deny ourselves. Through this petition, we have new thoughts and a new mind, and guided by the Holy Spirit, we learn things that please God, and we desire them. In other words, this petition fits together with our sanctification, in which we walk in the guidance of the Holy Spirit and subject our entire selves to God.

The first petition in the second part (and therefore the fourth petition in the prayer), "give us this day our daily bread" (Mt 6:11), teaches us to ask God to provide for the needs of our bodies. This petition is not just about food and clothing in themselves but also all the means that will enable us to have food and clothing and other necessities in life. In other words, in this petition, we throw ourselves completely on God's care and mercy and ask God to take care of us daily.[22] Asking God to provide for our physical needs does not at all mean that we consider our bodies more important than our souls. Calvin says that even though the forgiveness of our sins is more important than our physical needs, Christ places the petition in this part of the prayer to teach us that when we have good nourishment and a good life, we can then do the other acts that the next two petitions in the prayer teach us.

The prayer teaches us to ask God to give our *daily* bread to prevent us from being greedy and from indulging our desire for an excessive lifestyle. When we have plenty, we tend to spend what we

---

[21]Calvin, *Institutes* III.20.43.
[22]Calvin, *Institutes* III.20.44.

have indiscriminately. Therefore, Christ teaches us to ask for the need of each day, to teach us that our Father, who provides for us today, will not fail to provide for us tomorrow. Even when we are rich in material possessions, we are still required to ask for our daily bread.

The next or the fifth petition, "forgive us our debts, as we also have forgiven our debtors" (Mt 6:12), teaches us what living in heaven really means. God's people are those who have been forgiven for all their sins. In our forgiven life God also prepares us to resist temptations.[23] Calvin takes the word *debts* to mean that when we sin, we owe God truth and righteousness. In sin we are unable to please God, and therefore we are to be punished for our sins. And we are never able to pay for our own debts to God. Only because of God's mercy are we forgiven from all the debts of sin. We owe our forgiveness to Christ, who has paid the ransom for our sins. And as we have received forgiveness from our sins, we are also called to forgive others who have done us wrong. This petition, however, does not mean that we can give pardon to others for their sins, because only God has the power to pardon people. We are called to forgive others in the sense that we do not hold hatred or grudges against them. We are also called to divert our desire for revenge on those who have done us ill. Therefore, we do not remember the wrongs that others have done because we voluntarily forget those wrongs. We do not have the right to ask God to forgive us if we do not forgive others. Calvin reminds us that the petition is not to be read conditionally, in the sense that we can only get forgiveness from God after we forgive others. Instead, Calvin says that the petition teaches us the certainty of our forgiveness, and as sure as God forgives our sins, we too are called to forgive others.

---

[23]Calvin, *Institutes* III.20.45.

The sixth petition, "and do not bring us to the time of trial, but rescue us from the evil one" (Mt 6:13), according to Calvin, is related to the fact that God has written his laws in our hearts. But because we often forget the law of God, the petition gives us a type of protection or armor so that we can have victory against the devil.[24] This petition is also a reminder that we need the Holy Spirit so we can have a heart of obedience that is directed only to God. There are many kinds of temptation. The depravity of our hearts leads us to trespass the law of God, which, ironically, has been written in our hearts. And things that are not necessarily evil can turn into temptation for us. Such temptation may take the form of wealth or fame. While wealth and fame in themselves are not evil, they can potentially cause us to be greedy, and in the process we are led away from God. With this petition as armor, we can be protected from these temptations, and we can stand firm against sin. As we pray that we are delivered from temptation, we are asking God to provide us with the full supply of his grace so that we triumph against the temptation that comes from the devil.

The conclusion of the prayer, "for the kingdom and the power and the glory are yours forever. Amen," indicates that God wants to give us a calm and certain assurance of our faith. Calvin is aware that this sentence was not included in some copies of the manuscripts of the Bible. But because it is in accord with the whole prayer, he includes it in his explication of the prayer.[25] Whoever we are, we need to pray. In our prayers, we are given the confidence that power, kingdom, and glory belong to God alone. And these will never depart from God.

The word *Amen* at the conclusion of the prayer is also important. "Amen" expresses the eagerness and assurance of certainty in our hearts that we will receive what we ask for. While we rest our hope

---

[24]Calvin, *Institutes* III.20.46.
[25]Calvin, *Institutes* III.20.47.

in God, we are full of confidence that God has given us our petitions. With the word *Amen*, the prayer is complete in all its parts. It is so complete that anything outside of the words of the prayer is impious.

Calvin considers the Lord's Prayer the ultimate pattern for all our prayers. We may say our prayers using different wording, but the fundamental content of our prayers should not depart from it. He points out that in Scripture there are many other prayers uttered to God, but because all of these prayers are guided by the same Spirit, they ultimately carry the message and truth of the Lord's Prayer. He holds the Lord's Prayer in such a high regard that he calls it "the teaching of divine wisdom."[26] Through this prayer God has taught us his will, and God wills all that is necessary.

Election and Predestination

Calvin discusses the doctrine of election and predestination toward the end of Book Three of the *Institutes*. The placement of this doctrine in this part of the book is worthy of our examination. As you recall, in Book Three Calvin discusses our justification by faith alone. Justification does not depend on our works and cannot be earned. The long discussion on how God justifies us and forgives our sins because of Christ's righteousness leads to a discussion on prayer, the way we communicate to God. Only after discussing all these important topics does Calvin deal with the doctrine of election and predestination. The placement of the discussion of this doctrine at this point in the book shows us that the doctrine of election and predestination is not a central dogma in Calvin's theology. As I have indicated earlier in this book, there are people who misunderstand Calvin's theology and say that election and predestination are the center of Calvin's theological thought and that he

---

[26]Calvin, *Institutes* III.20.49.

builds his entire theological system on these doctrines. This is not a good reading of Calvin's *Institutes*. It is clear to careful readers that Calvin discusses the doctrine to show that because salvation is not dependent on our own work but fully on God's grace to us, then our justification or salvation comes out of God's ultimate authority as God. It is God's decision to save us. Therefore, our salvation lies entirely in the fact that God has chosen us in Christ before the foundation of the world. To put it differently, I would like to point out that, in Calvin's mind, the doctrines of election and predestination are the natural, logical reasoning regarding our salvation. This doctrine comes toward the end of the long explanation of the knowledge of God the Creator and Redeemer, our creation in the image of God and our fallenness because of our sins, and our salvation by the grace of God only. Then, once we know that God is the sovereign God, who in his goodness is willing to save us, our salvation is securely guaranteed because God has chosen us.

In explaining the doctrine of election, Calvin points us to the simple reality that the good news of the gospel is not preached equally to everyone in the world. And people who have heard the gospel do not always respond to it in the same way. Calvin attributes this reality to the fact that our salvation lies deep in God's incomprehensible judgment, in which God chooses whom he saves. God gives salvation to some and destruction to others. Here Calvin talks about a doctrine that his followers later call the doctrine of double predestination, in which God offers salvation to some and denies it to others. Calvin acknowledges that this reality is not an easy doctrine. The only way to understand this doctrine, according to him, is by understanding well that salvation flows from God's free mercy. When we pay close attention to this doctrine, we give honor to God's glory and are made humble, because we understand that our salvation flows directly from God and not from us. God is sovereign, and he saves people out of his good pleasure. Because the election of our salvation comes directly from God's judgment, we can be fully assured that it is good. Even when we do not have all the answers to the question of why God elects some to eternal salvation and others to damnation, we can rely on God's goodness and believe that everything God does is good. We cannot fathom God's goodness. What we can do is hold on to the conviction that God's good pleasure will bring an end that is eternally good.

Calvin finds the foundation of this doctrine in Scripture. In the book of Genesis we read that God chose and called Abraham to be the father of God's own people (Gen 12:1-3). The election of Abraham continued with Israel, whom God made into his own nation.[27] Paul teaches, in the passage of Romans 11, that in the present age there are remnants of those who are chosen by grace and that God elects those he predestined. If God chooses people to salvation by grace, then salvation is clearly not by works. Furthermore, Paul clearly states that only when we understand salvation as attributable only to undeserved election can we know God saves the ones he wills out of his own good pleasure to save.[28] In the Gospel of John, we read Jesus' statement that he promises safety to all whom the Father has brought into his keeping (Jn 10:28-29).

The topic of predestination is not easy. It is made even more complicated by people's uncontrolled curiosity in the doctrine. To prevent misunderstanding, Calvin reminds us that when we talk about the doctrine, we must remember that we are trying to get into the depths of God's wisdom. If we proceed too boldly, we risk falling into a labyrinth that we cannot get out of. Because the doctrine lies hidden in God's mind, we are not to pry into the doctrine too much. God's glory will shine brighter when we are willing to surrender ourselves to God's wisdom. What God has told us in Scripture is enough for us. We are allowed to know about the

---

[27]Calvin, *Institutes* III.21.5.
[28]Calvin, *Institutes* III.21.7.

doctrine as much as Scripture tells us, yet this does not mean that we are to avoid discussing the doctrine altogether. There is a balance between limiting ourselves to Scripture's teaching and discussing the doctrine under the guidance of the Holy Spirit. Based on the teaching of the Bible, Calvin explains predestination thus:

> God once established by his eternal and unchangeable plan those whom he long before determined once for all to receive into his salvation, and those whom, on the other hand, he would devote to destruction. We assert that with respect to the elect, this plan was founded upon his freely given mercy, without regard to human worth.[29]

In Calvin's time there were people who tried to explain predestination by way of what they called the foreknowledge of God. Calvin disagrees with this explanation. These people said that God grants people their salvation based on their merit. In eternity God has the foreknowledge of those who will have the merits to earn salvation, and therefore God saves them because of those merits. As for those who will be bent toward evil, God will then condemn them to punishment. Calvin's disagreement with this view is that it still relies on good works.

Furthermore, basing his argument on Paul's teaching, Calvin vehemently states that good works never have any place in our salvation and that the view of divine foreknowledge should be rejected. Paul teaches that God has saved us and called us to a holy life not because of anything we have done but because of God's own grace that he has given to us before the beginning of time (2 Tim 1:9). Paul's statement that we are called to be holy is the key for Calvin to reject the view of foreknowledge. When people say that God could foresee those who would be holy and therefore God would

---

[29]Calvin, *Institutes* III.21.7.

elect them, those people reverse the order Paul uses in this passage. As Calvin explains, Paul says that God has elected us to make us holy, not that God elected us because he saw that we would be holy. When we say that believers are elected that they may be holy, we must say that holiness has its beginning in election and not the reverse. Our election, Calvin reiterates, cannot be based on the future good works that God saw in any individual. When Christ says, "You did not choose me but I chose you" (Jn 15:16), he did not just exclude past merits but also taught that we do not have anything in ourselves through which we could be chosen.

Election happens through God's calling. As the hearts of the elect are softened after they hear God's call, those of the wicked are blinded and hardened. Even though the calling is given to all people equally, the promise of salvation is not given universally or equally. Therefore, not all people who hear the calling or the preaching of the gospel will accept the good news of the gospel.[30] In this regard Calvin sees two kinds of callings, namely general and special callings. General calling is the one extended to everyone through the preaching of the Word of God. This calling is given to both the elect and the non-elect. Special calling, on the other hand, is targeted to the elect alone. Through the inward illumination of the Holy Spirit, the Word of God dwells in the hearts of the elect and this calling brings the elect to repentance.[31]

Satan often attacks believers, causing them to doubt their election and leading them astray by looking for answers outside of the Word of God. Calvin understands that from time to time we may wonder about our election. However, when this thought dominates our minds, it will cause terrible torment and mental confusion, taking away the peace and rest we find in God alone. We must avoid such questioning as far as we can. Calvin urges believers

---

[30]Calvin, *Institutes* III.24.1.
[31]Calvin, *Institutes* III.24.8.

to fully rest in God alone and to have the comfort of predestination in God, who has elected us from all eternity. God has adopted us to be his children. This is a clear testimony of Scripture. When we look at the doctrine of predestination and election from this angle, we find our rest and comfort. The purpose of our election, Calvin firmly says, is in the fact that we are adopted as the sons and daughters of God through Christ. We will inherit eternal salvation through God's favor.

Following Paul's teaching in Ephesians 1:4-5, Calvin assures us that those whom God has adopted as his children, God elected not for themselves but only in Christ. Calvin believes that God our Father can only love us in Christ, and because of Christ, we are honored with the inheritance of his kingdom. We are grafted into the body of Christ, and we therefore become one with Christ. This way we are assured that our names are written in the book of life. We can see the effect of this doctrine in our prayers. When we pray, we do not start with the question whether we are elect. Rather, we pray because we are already assured that we have been saved and satisfied with God's own promises. We come to him in prayer, and we do not try to find our help from anything other than God our Father.

Those who have been elected in Christ receive the full assurance that God cares for us eternally. This certainty is confirmed through Christ who has done the work of redemption for our sakes. Jesus has promised that he is our great Shepherd (Jn 10:2-3), and this means that he keeps us safe forever. Therefore, we can lay hold of Christ, who has loved us so much that he offered himself for our salvation. Therefore, Christ frees us from the anxiety of our perseverance. Jesus, who has given us salvation, can never lose our salvation. Jesus promises that those whom the Father has given to him will never be snatched away from him (Jn 10:27-29). In this promise of Christ, Calvin lays the foundation for the security of our salvation. We will never lose our salvation because it is guaranteed by Christ.

In our daily experience, we often find people we thought belonged to Christ, but later they turn away from him. Is this a case in which people lost their salvation? Calvin addresses this issue by saying that these people, even though they seemingly were in Christ, were never actually united with Christ. They are of the same group as the children of perdition. These people, though they demonstrate some similarities to the elect, do not have the assurance of salvation that the elect have. Calvin reminds us that we should not use these people as proof that we could lose our salvation and thereby lack confidence in the assurance that God has given us.

Calvin addresses a couple of biblical passages that, read superficially, may sound contradictory to the doctrine of election and predestination. The first passage is Ezekiel 33:11: "Say to them, As I live, says the Lord GOD, I have no pleasure in the death of the wicked, but that the wicked turn from their ways and live; turn back, turn back from your evil ways; for why will you die, O house of Israel?" If God says that he does not take pleasure in the death of the wicked, why would he choose people for damnation? Calvin explains that the context of this passage is God's readiness to forgive Israel as soon as they repent. When sinners repent, Calvin says, God will not punish them. This passage, therefore, is about God, who wills the repentance of those whom he invites to himself.[32]

The other passage that needs some explanation regarding election and predestination is 1 Timothy 2:3-4: "This is right and is acceptable in the sight of God our Savior, who desires everyone to be saved and to come to the knowledge of the truth." If Paul says that God wants everyone to be saved, some people may say, then God will not elect people for damnation, as the doctrine of double predestination maintains. Calvin replies by showing that this passage must be understood in the larger context of what Paul

---

[32]Calvin, *Institutes* III.24.15.

writes. Here, Paul instructs Timothy to pray earnestly for all classes of people, including kings and rulers. At that time Timothy was leading the church in Ephesus, where not all the civil leaders believed in Jesus. Therefore, it seemed absurd to pray for rulers who would not really follow God's commands. In this letter Paul was assuring Timothy that such prayer is nonetheless acceptable to the Lord, who wills all people to be saved. What Paul means, says Calvin, is that God has not closed the way of salvation for any class or group of people, including kings and rulers.[33]

The teaching of election and predestination brings us to the hope of our ultimate glory, namely the final resurrection. As believers, we are said to have passed from death into life, just as Jesus died and has risen from the dead. All discussions of salvation lead us to look toward heaven, where Christ is. We will only be able to share the benefits of Christ when we lift our minds to the resurrection, just as Christ has been resurrected. Calvin invites us to strive toward resurrection because if our minds are only bound to the world, we will always suffer from our exhaustion from the world. Paul has said that if Christ was not resurrected from the dead, the entire gospel is false (1 Cor 15:13-17). Our condition would be worse than those of the non-believers, and the power of the gospel would be completely lost. But in true union with Christ, we have hope. Our body will be made conformable to the body of our head, Jesus Christ. Whenever we think about resurrection, we must always think about Jesus our Savior, who, having completed his human life, gained immortality. Jesus is the pledge of our future resurrection.

Scripture attests that Christ is now in heaven, and one day he will come as judge.[34] On that day our vile bodies will be changed to be like the glorious body of the resurrected Christ (Phil 3:20-21). Calvin intends that the teaching of our resurrection become the

---

[33]Calvin, *Institutes* III.24.16.
[34]Calvin, *Institutes* III.25.1.

backbone of our faith. Christ rose again so that we can share with him in eternal life. In teaching about our final resurrection, Calvin goes back to God the Trinity. God the Father raised Jesus the Son from the dead, and Jesus was raised by the power of the Holy Spirit. The Holy Spirit also will raise us from dead.[35] The resurrection of Christ functions as a mirror for us, because in it we can see our own resurrection, and thus we have proof for our minds that we too will be resurrected. And as we still live here on earth, we should not be tired of waiting, because the timing is not ours but God's alone. We must rest in him and wait until he brings his kingdom in his time.

In Book Three of the *Institutes* taken as a whole, Calvin shows how we can be saved. In line with the most foundational beliefs of the Reformation, Calvin clearly argues that salvation is by grace alone, through faith alone. Our salvation does not require good works on our part. The Holy Spirit unites us with Christ, and that is how we receive salvation. The beauty of Calvin's doctrine of salvation lies in his view of double grace, namely that in our salvation we receive justification and sanctification. By placing his discussion on prayer *after* that of justification and sanctification, Calvin indicates that prayer is a natural expression of thanksgiving and our petitions to God *after* we are saved and as we live in a sanctified relationship with God in the power of the Holy Spirit. Following his explication of the Lord's Prayer, he discusses the doctrines of election and predestination, signaling that these two doctrines are important but are not the center of his entire theological system. He ends Book Three with a deep theological look at the final resurrection, the most joyful event that believers are waiting for. Christ rose again from the dead so that we can live in his company eternally.

---

[35]Calvin, *Institutes* III.25.3.

Suggestions for Further Reading

Billings, J. Todd, and I. John Hesselink, eds. *Calvin's Theology and Its Reception: Disputes, Development, and New Possibilities*. Louisville, KY: Westminster John Knox, 2012.

Jones, Serene. *Calvin and the Rhetoric of Piety*. Louisville, KY: Westminster John Knox, 1995.

Muller, Richard A. *Unaccommodated Calvin: Studies in the Foundation of a Theological Tradition*. New York: Oxford University Press, 2000.

Venema, Cornelius P. *Accepted and Renewed in Christ: The "Twofold Grace of God" and the Interpretation of Calvin's Theology*. Göttingen: Vandenhoeck & Ruprecht, 2015.

- 9 -

Book Four of the *Institutes*

Finally, in Book Four, Calvin shows how God provides the outward means to support and uphold us as we live from day to day following him. God knows that even though we have received the unspeakable joy of salvation, given to us through the redemption Christ has accomplished, we are often lazy and ungrateful. And so God gives us the church, which is God's instrument, provided so that the people of God can continue to grow in their faith.

The Church

The church, according to Calvin, nurtures us in faith. Reinterpreting the famous saying of Cyprian (AD 210–258), an early Christian author, Calvin reminds his readers that as God is our Father, the church is our mother.[1] Calvin wants his readers to know that the church has the role of taking care of people, similarly to how a mother cares for and raises her children. He explains, based on Galatians 4:26, that we are the children of the new heavenly Jerusalem. In calling the church our mother, Calvin implies that the church has an important role in ensuring that people receive proper care, instruction, and in a way discipline. The opening paragraph of

---

[1]John Calvin, *Institutes of the Christian Religion* [1559], ed. John T. McNeill, trans. Ford Lewis Battles (Philadelphia: Westminster, 1960), IV.1.1.

the fourth book of the *Institutes* lays a foundation for the topic that he discusses in the rest of the book.

> Calvin distinguishes the invisible from the visible church. The former is the people of God of all ages and from all places who will be gathered together in God's presence. Its members are all God's elect from the creation of the world until its end. The latter is the church in the here and now, where people physically meet to worship God. It is the church as an institution. Calvin wrote: "Sometimes by the term 'church' it means that which is actually in God's presence, into which no persons are received but those who are children of God by grace of adoption and true members of Christ by sanctification of the Holy Spirit.... Often, however, the name 'church' designates the whole multitude of men spread over the earth who profess to worship one God and Christ.... In this church are mingled many hypocrites who have nothing of Christ but the name and outward appearance." (*Institutes,* IV.1.7)

Calvin believes that there are two types of church, namely the visible and the invisible church. The visible church is the church in which we worship, participate, and serve. It is the church in our time and our place. In the visible church, people go to church services, hear sermons, celebrate the sacraments, profess their beliefs, and share love with one another. The invisible church, on the other hand, refers to all God's elect people of all times and places. Its members are the people from the past, present, and future. When we say that the church is universal or catholic, this is what we mean. The invisible church is the one church, the people who belong to God and have been redeemed by Christ. The church is one body, united by one baptism. They live in one hope, faith, and love. Not only are the people called into one inheritance of eternal life, but they also participate in one God and one Christ. But, Calvin notes, not all members of the visible church are members of the invisible church, though it is not for us to know who truly belongs.

Calvin explains the meaning of the church by following what the creed says: "I believe in the church, the communion of saints."[2] The church is the communion of saints because the church is the gathering of God's people who have been redeemed, and therefore made holy, by the redemption that Christ has won. The saints, or the society of the redeemed people who belong to God, receive equally all the benefits that God has conferred on all of them. In turn, all the people share these benefits. That is why the church is called the communion of the saints. The benefit that God gives to the church is that salvation is sure and secure: no matter what happens in the world, the saints will not lose their salvation, because God is the one working for their salvation. The church stands on God's election, and therefore it cannot waver or move. And it is joined in the steadfastness of Christ, who will never allow his people to be taken away from him.

The title "mother" for the visible church is important. As members of the visible church, people must remain with their mother for proper upbringing. As a mother, the church has the duty to educate the members, and in return, the members must also be willing to be educated by the church. In the relationship between the members and the church as their mother, we also see the fatherly love of God. This love is poured out by way of the church. Therefore, leaving or abandoning the visible church is a fatal action. One cannot receive God's love without being in communion with one's mother, the visible church.[3]

---

[2]Calvin, *Institutes* IV.1.2.
[3]Calvin, *Institutes* IV.1.4.

Visible churches include both the true church and false ones. The marks of the true church are the pure ministry of the Word of God and the pure celebration of the sacraments.[4] Calvin acknowledges that one church may have slightly different doctrinal beliefs from others. Doctrinal teachings do not hold equal importance for all people. Some doctrines are of the utmost importance and therefore are nonnegotiable, such as the belief in one God, that God is the Trinity, that salvation is only through the work of Christ, and that we are only saved by the grace of God. But true believers may believe different things about other controversial doctrines, such as what will happen to the soul when one dies. Matters that are nonessential should not be a reason to fight among Christians. However, Calvin insists that to evaluate whether a church is true, we must see if the church truthfully preaches the Word of God and celebrates the sacraments purely.

The Apostles' Creed tells us that the church is holy. The fact that the church is holy does not mean that it is perfect. It is holy because Christ makes it holy. Daily, Christ smooths out all the wrinkles that the church has. The holiness of the church is a process that progresses steadily, but it is not a state of perfection. Calvin believes that the Lord has never been without his church, and never will be until the end of time. Even though the world has been tainted by the sin of Adam, God has always worked for the sanctification—or the process of making holy—of his church. Therefore, each generation in the entire history of the world—and of the church—is never without God's mercy. Calvin refers to biblical verses that talk about God's faithfulness in his covenantal relationship with his people such as Psalm 89:3, Psalm 132:13-14, and Jeremiah 31:31-33 as a way to explain that God has always worked for the church to sanctify it.

---

[4]Calvin, *Institutes* IV.1.9.

Forgiveness of sin is God's way of making the church holy. God's mercy is given constantly to sinners because otherwise, it would be futile. Believers are aware of all their failures to obey God, and therefore they need God's mercy. God has called his people into eternal salvation, therefore the people must always remember that pardon from sin is readily available. When we become members of Christ's body, we know that our sins have been forgiven daily because of God's goodness and generosity. Pardon from sin is through the merits of Christ only by the sanctification performed by the Holy Spirit. In teaching about the holiness of the church, Calvin shows a contrast between his view and that of the medieval church. In the medieval church people were taught that they needed to get indulgences so that they could reduce their time in purgatory. Calvin rejects every notion of purgatorial sanctification. He shows his readers that the sanctifying work of the Holy Spirit, based on the redemptive work of Christ that stems from the mercy of God, is enough to make us, the church, holy.

God ordains leaders in the church to guide the people to live according to God's Word. Calvin states that God does not need the help of human beings to guide the church. But the fact that God uses people to lead shows us God's character. First, he is willing to go to the level of human beings, using them as his ambassadors to interpret his Word. Second, he teaches us to live in humility because he wants us to obey his Word, even as it is preached by our fellow human beings. Following Paul's teaching in Ephesians 4:4-16, Calvin explains that God uses ministers and teachers in the church to maintain the bond of unity among God's people. These leaders are also protectors and guardians of the church.

Critique Against the False Church

From time to time in the *Institutes*, Calvin takes a polemical tone against the teachings and beliefs of the Roman Catholic Church of his time. As I have mentioned before, he can accept minor doctrinal differences between churches of different groups. However, he points out the major errors of the Church of Rome so that his readers do not fall into those errors. He cannot tolerate the overturn of essential doctrines of the church, especially when the sacraments are abused and the Word of God is not truthfully preached. The church is founded on the teaching of the prophets and the apostles, Calvin believes, and this means that the church should be firmly built upon the Word of God—the Old and the New Testaments, where the teaching of salvation in Christ is written.

The Church of Rome in his time, or "the Papacy," as Calvin often calls it, had been severely mistaken. Instead of the true ministry of the Word, the Roman Catholic Church operated under a corrupt government that was built on lies. In Calvin's judgment, that church had partly excluded itself from God's pure light. In place of the Lord's Supper, it practiced sacrilege. The worship of God was taken away and replaced with a Mass that was full of superstitions. According to Calvin, the Church of Rome had buried crucial Christian doctrines, and public services became the hotbed of idolatry and profanity. Then the church used its power to excommunicate the people who disagreed with its practices. Calvin criticizes the Church of Rome's declaration that it was the only church, as if there were no other church. He notes that the Church of Rome had a stronghold in Italy, Spain, and France, and he laments the fact that France, his homeland, was greatly influenced by the teaching of the Roman Catholic Church. He criticizes Rome's claim that it adhered closely to the teachings of the early Christian teachers such as Irenaeus, Tertullian, Origen, Augustine, and many others, while in fact it had failed to be true to their teachings.

Calvin states that the corruption under the Papacy was comparable to that in the time of Israel under King Jeroboam (1 Kings 12). The church was as idolatrous as Israel had been.[5] However, even though the Papacy was not the true church, it demanded that the people do two acts. First, the people must participate in all its prayers, sacraments, and ceremonies. Second, they must give the church every honor, power, and authority that Christ has handed out to his church. Calvin argues that the Papacy did not rightly minister the Word of God, and therefore it was not to be counted as the true church. He shows that the practices of the ancient church were not exactly the same as those of Rome in the time just before the Reformation, even though Rome claimed that it had always been faithful to the practice of the ancient church.

Calvin devotes chapters four to twelve of Book Four of the *Institutes* to demonstrating how Rome had not been the true church. He demonstrates that the teachings and practices of the ancient church were good and faithful to the Word of God, but the Papacy of his time had abused them badly. He takes time to reveal that church leaders had become immoral and lustful, that bishops and presbyters had misused the church's money, and that the church had mishandled power in many ways.

At the center of the abuse is Rome's interpretation of Matthew 16:16-20. In this passage, when Jesus asked the disciples who the Son of Man was, Peter said that he was the Messiah, the Son of the living God. When Jesus heard Peter's statement, he said that on that rock he would build his church, and to Peter he gave the key to the kingdom of heaven; whatever was loosed on earth would be loosed in heaven, and whatever was bound on earth would be bound in heaven. For a long time, the Church of Rome held that Jesus was

---

[5]Calvin, *Institutes* IV.2.9.

building his church on Peter, "the rock," and because the bishops of Rome were Peter's successors, they also held the power of the keys that Jesus gave to Peter. Rome's explanation was that the Papacy had the power to forgive or not to forgive sins. This power included the power to excommunicate people from the church. Calvin disagrees with this interpretation. He says that the only true head of the church is Christ. The church cannot have a human head, and therefore the pope—the successor of Peter according to Rome—is not the head of the church. Calvin then goes through the long history of the church to expose many of the cases in the church where popes of the past had been proved to do wrong. He insists that Rome had failed to be obedient to God.

Church Discipline

Calvin sees that the church has the authority to govern the way people must respond to the Word of God to live their Christian lives. He believes the church must act within its power to maintain discipline for the people. He understands that people do not like the idea of discipline, but he believes that discipline is necessary to lead people to follow the teaching of Scripture faithfully. Christians must live daily in obedience to God. Without discipline, they will not be able to fulfill their responsibilities as Christians. No society or household can operate well without discipline, he maintains. The same is true for the church. He likens discipline to the sinews that hold all parts of the body together, whereas the doctrine of salvation in Christ alone is the lifeblood of the church, the body of Christ.

The church cannot allow any person to teach any doctrine as they wish. The preaching of God's Word must be done in an orderly manner and be truthful to the Word. All who teach others must do so carefully and honestly, taking any measure possible to ensure that their teaching is kept true. To achieve all this, therefore, the church needs discipline. The purpose of church discipline is to prevent people from attacking the teaching of Christ. At times, discipline can also function as a father's stern punishment to a wayward child. The father does this not because he hates the child but, on the contrary, because he loves him. In the same way, church discipline functions as a loving punishment for believers who have sinned. The church would be chaotic without discipline.

The first—and perhaps the most important—element of discipline is private rebuke. When church members find that a brother or a sister has sinned, they must talk privately and directly to the brother or sister, reminding them of God's Word and the need to repent. Pastors, too, must be keen in observing the members of the church, and when they find that a member has committed sin or wrongdoing, they must rebuke the member in private. The call for pastors, according to Calvin, involves the responsibility to remind people when they do wrong according to Scripture. When a wrongdoer has been privately reminded and rebuked but persists in sin, he or she will then face banishment from the company of believers.[6]

Calvin distinguishes private from public sins. Private sins are sins that we do in our hearts, the wrongdoings that only God and we know. But there are sins that others can see. He takes Jesus' teaching in Matthew 18:15, "If another member of the church sins against you, go and point out the fault when the two of you are alone. If the member listens to you, you have regained that one," to mean that we have the capacity to know of certain sins that people do, especially the ones that are done against us. For such public sins, Calvin takes Paul's instruction to Timothy in 1 Timothy 5:20 that these sins are to be rebuked publicly. Taking another example from Paul when he rebuked Peter openly in Galatians 2:14, Calvin further

---

[6]Calvin, *Institutes* IV.12.2.

emphasizes that there are times when the church must rebuke public sins publicly.

There are three reasons why the church needs to exercise discipline, or purposes for doing so. First, church discipline maintains the glory of God. People who claim to be Christians but continue sinning insult God and his church. The church should not provide a safe haven for a conspiracy of wicked people. As the body of Christ, the church should not be disgraced. This principle is closely connected to the celebration of the Lord's Supper. The Supper is holy, and therefore it should not be partaken by those who are not worthy of it. Therefore, the practice of church discipline is closely connected to prohibiting those who are being disciplined from eating and drinking the Lord's Supper. The second purpose is to protect good people in the church from being tainted by bad ones. Calvin takes Paul's instructions to the church in Corinth as his strong argument that the church must take any step necessary to protect the faithful from people who are immoral, deceitful, and plain sinful. The third purpose is for sinners to repent and, through their repentance, to remain in their saving relationship with Christ. Therefore, the intention of church discipline is not to cast people out or away from salvation. Even though excommunication as a form of church discipline punishes the person for a period of time, it does so in such a way to prevent the person from the eternal damnation the person would face if not excommunicated and therefore never repented.

Calvin explains how Christians must follow the teaching of the Bible as an expression of their obedience to God. Fasting, praying, and other spiritual disciplines can be beneficial for the spiritual lives of the people. He reminds Christians, however, that they do not do them superstitiously. He criticizes the Church of Rome, which told the people to refrain from eating meat during Lent only for the sake of not eating meat, without providing people with good theological teaching behind the meaning of such fasting. In this case Lent observance became a burden and would not lead the people into true devotion to God.

The clergy, of all people, must faithfully follow a disciplined life. Since ancient times, the church had strict regulations for clergy.[7] They were strictly prohibited from hunting, gambling, partying, practicing usury, dancing, and many other activities. The main point behind clergy discipline, says Calvin, is that clergy are expected to lead the people not just by words but also by their example of upright conduct. He laments the fact that the clergy of the Church of Rome in his time had fallen away from living disciplined lives. He is saddened by the abuses committed by many clergymen. In the section of the *Institutes* where he criticizes clergy who are not disciplined, Calvin also criticizes the practice of clerical celibacy imposed by Rome on its clergymen. He is adamant in emphasizing that clerical celibacy is not biblical at all. He firmly believes that Christ sees marriage as worthy of honor. He boldly states, therefore, that forbidding clergymen from getting married is a tyranny not just against God's Word but also against the equity of all people.

The Sacraments

What are the sacraments, and what role do they play in the Christian life? Such questions led to intense debate and controversy during the Reformation. According to Calvin, the sacraments are aids that God provides for his people to strengthen their faith. Sacraments work closely together with the preaching of God's Word. Calvin defines sacraments as "an outward sign by which the Lord seals on our consciences the promises of his good will toward us in order to sustain the weakness of our faith; and we in turn attest our piety

---

[7]Calvin, *Institutes* IV.12.22.

toward him."[8] Or to put it more simply, the sacraments are testimonies of God's grace for his people, confirmed by outward signs for us to attest to God in piety.

The sacraments are closely connected to the promise of salvation that God made to his people in the past. They function as the confirmation of the promise. While God's truth is strong, our faith is weak and therefore needs strengthening from all directions. The sacraments work as a type of mechanism that God provides to make our faith strong. In the sacraments, the ordinary objects—water in baptism, and bread and wine in the Lord's Supper—convey the deeper promise of God. Following Augustine, Calvin emphasizes that the Word of God must accompany the sacraments, because otherwise, the sacraments will not have any meaning. As the confirmation of God's promise to his people, the sacraments function as the seal of the promise, just as in the Old Testament God's covenants with his people were accompanied by a sign that sealed the covenant. Following what Paul wrote in Romans 4:11, Calvin explains that in the covenant between God and Abraham, circumcision was the sign of the covenant and the seal of the righteousness that Abraham had by faith. Just as any legal document requires a seal to make it binding, the sacraments work as a seal to the covenant between God and human beings.

The sacraments also need the work of the Holy Spirit to fulfill their functions. Without the Holy Spirit, they mean nothing. The Holy Spirit is the power behind the sacraments. When the Holy Spirit works in us, our work or ministry to others becomes meaningful and powerful. Similarly, only when the Holy Spirit is present in the sacraments can they perform their intended function. God nourishes us through the sacraments. However, we must also remember that our confidence is not in the sacraments. Their only

---

[8]Calvin, *Institutes* IV.14.1.

task is to make God's promise visible to us. In themselves they do not have power. Calvin disagrees with the teaching of the Church of Rome that believed the sacraments themselves are God's grace. The church has a saying in Latin, *ex opere operato*, which in English can be literally translated as "by the work worked." This is a belief that the act of administering the sacraments itself works to bring grace to the people. According to this concept, the sacraments work like magic, as though they had the secret powers that would bring God's grace to the people or save people from sin. Calvin strongly disagrees with this idea. He states that assurance of salvation does not depend on human participation in the sacraments. Christ is the substance of the sacraments; they do not promise anything apart from him. Therefore, the sacraments have the same task as the preaching of the Word of God, namely, to give Christ to us, and together with him is all the goodness of heaven that God has prepared for his people.

Baptism. What is the role of baptism? During the Reformation, the sacrament of baptism became a matter of controversy. The vast majority of Christians—Catholic and Protestant—practiced infant baptism, but the Anabaptists rejected it. Just as he wanted to distinguish his theology from the Anabaptists on other points, so too Calvin wanted to show his readers that he affirmed the importance of baptism, including infant baptism. Calvin calls baptism "the sacrament of initiation by which we are received into the society of the church."[9] In baptism God's children are grafted into Christ so that they may become one with him, to grow in him and to be nourished by him. Baptism has three functions. First, it is a token of our cleansing from our sins. Second, it signifies our dying and rising with Christ. Paul teaches us that we have been baptized into Christ's death that we may walk in the newness of life (Rom 6:3-4).

---

[9]Calvin, *Institutes* IV.15.1.

In baptism we die in the mortification of the flesh, and we rise again in the vivification of the spirit. Third, baptism unites us with Christ so that we share all the blessings that Christ has.

Calvin defends the theology of infant baptism. He finds the biblical foundation of infant baptism in the covenant between God and Abraham in Genesis 17, in which God gave circumcision as the sign of the covenant. The most important point in God's covenant with Abraham and his descendants is that God promises to be their God, and they become God's people. Similarly, in baptizing infants, the church shows God's covenantal promise to the people. Calvin states that this promise includes the promise of eternal life in Christ, who is the son of Abraham. Just as much as circumcision was given to baby boys when they were eight days old as the sign of the covenant, baptism is also given to infants as the sign of God's covenant to his people.

The sign that God gives to the infants in their baptisms is also a confirmation of God's promise to the believing parents. In baptism God tells the parents that, just as much as God loves them, he also loves their children. In the sacrament of baptism, the parents—as well as the rest of the congregation of the church—receive the strengthening of their faith. At the same time, the children also draw direct benefit from their baptism. They are received into the church. And as they are received, they also benefit other members of the church by expanding the church family. As they grow up, they serve God in the church because they have received the formal sign of adoption into the family of God in their baptism. Here is how he puts it:

> If anyone should object that the promise ought to be enough to confirm the salvation of our children, I disregard this argument. For God views this otherwise; as he perceives our weakness, so he has willed to deal tenderly with us in this

matter. Accordingly, let those who embrace the promise that God's mercy is to be extended to their children deem it their duty to offer them to the church to be sealed by the symbol of mercy, and thereby to arouse themselves to a surer confidence, because they see with their very eyes the covenant of the Lord engraved upon the bodies of their children.[10]

The Lord's Supper. And what is the role of the Lord's Supper? One of the most intense debates during the Reformation concerned the sacrament of the Lord's Supper, specifically the question whether and how Christ is present in the sacrament. As Calvin outlines his theology of the Lord's Supper, he sets his view apart from both the Roman Catholic view and the views of other Protestants.

After we are welcomed into the family of God in baptism, God does not treat us as servants. He treats us as his children. As a kind and graceful parent, God provides for us generously. Through Jesus Christ, God gives us another sacrament in the form of a spiritual feast in which Christ himself is the living bread on which our souls feed to have the eternal life (Jn 6:51). The signs of the sacrament, the bread and wine, symbolize the spiritual nourishment that we receive from the body and the blood of Christ. After grafting us into the body of Christ, God gives us food and drink so that we can grow in him. In the Lord's Supper, God invites us to meet him so that through the sacrament we can gain strength to live in this world until we see him in heaven.

The mystery of the union between Christ and us is invisible. Therefore, God gives us a sign that we can see in the bread and wine so that every time we celebrate the Lord's Supper, we remember that we are fed by Christ in our spirit just as much as our bodies are fed through bread and wine. In this mystical blessing, we receive

---

[10]Calvin, *Institutes* IV.16.9.

assurance that Christ once sacrificed his body and shed his blood for our salvation. Today, when we eat the bread and drink the wine, we realize the usefulness of Christ's sacrifice for our salvation. Christ instructs us to eat and drink the Supper, and this means that as partakers of the sacrament, we can experience the efficacy of his death for us. The covenant of salvation that Christ performed in his body and blood is renewed in the sacrament and continued as a confirmation of our faith every time we celebrate it.

Celebrating the Lord's Supper is a joyous occasion because in it we have a proof that we are a part of the body of Christ. As his body, we have the assurance that everything that belongs to him also belongs to us. Just as Christ has eternal life, we too have it. We can no longer be condemned by our sins because he has forgiven us from all our guilt. Because Christ has descended to earth, we can ascend to heaven. Communion, or the Lord's Supper, enables us to see that as much as Christ was physically present on earth to be seen and touched by people long ago, we are having communion with him now. His body has been given for our redemption, and now we have his redemption in us. The sacrament, according to Calvin, reminds us that we must always feed on Christ. Christ has become the source of life for us because he was born as a human, died, and rose again.

Calvin reminds his readers of two faults in understanding the sacrament. The first is that we separate the act of eating and drinking from the meaning behind it. He criticizes those who say that eating the bread and drinking the wine are nothing more than believing in Christ himself, or remembering what he has done for us, as affirmed by the Zwinglians. The second fault is that people think too much of the bread and the wine, to the point that they believe the actual or physical body and blood of Christ are present in the sacrament, as affirmed by both the Roman Catholics and the Lutherans, though in different ways. The former affirmed the doctrine of transubstantiation, according to which the substance of the bread and wine is completely changed into the body and blood of Christ, who is therefore bodily present. By comparison, the latter affirmed that Christ is bodily and really present, though not by transubstantiation but rather because both the bread and the body (or the wine and the blood) of Christ are present.

According to Calvin's view, the body and the blood of Christ truly feed our souls. The sign will not mean anything if it does not bring us to the actual reality. When we eat the bread and drink the wine, Christ is truly present there, by the great power of the Holy Spirit. Calvin insists that Christ's body does not come down in the bread and the wine. However, when we partake in the Lord's Supper, we are carried to heaven with our eyes and minds, so that we can see Christ and his glory in his kingdom. Physically, Christ has ascended to heaven to be seated at the right hand of God the Father, which means that he reigns supremely in his kingdom. Because the kingdom of God is not physical in nature but spiritual, Christ is also present in his Spirit at the Lord's Supper.[11] The Holy Spirit really unites us with Christ, even though we are separated from him by space. Christ brings his life to us in Communion. Then he seals his truth in it. Paul writes, "The cup of blessing that we bless, is it not a sharing in the blood of Christ? The bread that we break, is it not a sharing in the body of Christ?" (1 Cor 10:16), and Calvin takes this verse to mean that Christ is spiritually present in the bread and wine. Calvin draws a close relationship between the sign and the thing signified. By believing that Christ is truly present in the sacrament by the Holy Spirit, we have strong assurance that the visible sign is the seal of the invisible gift from God.

Words cannot explain the mystery of the process of the spiritual presence of Christ in the bread and wine of Communion. Here is

---

[11]Calvin, *Institutes* IV.17.18.

where faith comes in. Calvin acknowledges that on this matter, he feels the presence of Christ instead of understanding it with his mind. The sacrament does not just give our minds absolute assurance of eternal life but also truthfully secures the immortality of our bodies, which have been made alive by Christ's immortal body.

Calvin further disagrees with the Mass as performed and taught by the Church of Rome. He argues that the Mass dishonors Christ in that it requires the human priests to perform the sacrifice of Christ every time the church celebrates it. We read in the Bible, he states, that Christ is the Great High Priest who has sacrificed himself for our salvation. The papists, on the other hand, substituted their priests for Christ. In addition, the Mass focuses on the sacrifice of Christ on the altar of the church every time it is celebrated. For Calvin, this has the same meaning as overthrowing the actual sacrifice that Christ has done on the cross, which he did once and for all. In the Mass, the church sacrifices Christ again and again every time it is performed, and this is an incorrect understanding of the work of redemption that Christ has done for us. As such, the Mass causes the people to forget the actual death and resurrection of Christ.

Besides rejecting the Mass in the Church of Rome, Calvin also rejects the other five sacraments that Rome affirmed. By the medieval era, the church had established seven sacraments: baptism, confirmation, penance, the Mass (or the Eucharist), marriage, ordination, and the last rites (or extreme unction). In light of their reading of Scripture, Protestants hold that there are only two sacraments: baptism and Communion. Calvin writes a long explanation rejecting the five others as sacraments.[12] His main argument is that these five are not authorized by the Word of God and not used in the early church.

---

[12]Calvin, *Institutes* IV.19.1-37.

Civil Government

How should the church relate to the state? Calvin ends the *Institutes* with a discussion on civil government. Following Augustine, he writes that Christians live in two distinct yet related spheres. The first one is the realm of spiritual government, in which God rules and Christ is the King of kings. The second is the realm of human government, under human monarchs or rulers. Even though the spiritual government under God takes primacy, the human or civil government is necessary and good. Calvin holds a positive view of civil government. He does not see it as inherently corrupt or polluted, having nothing to do with Christians. He disagrees with some Christian groups who say that, because Christ teaches peace, civil government is inherently evil since a government goes to war. On the contrary, he argues, the kingdom of Christ and civil government can work together, though they are different spheres. He sees that the most important task of civil government is to ensure that people can freely worship God and that the government defends the true doctrine of the church so that human beings can live in peace and maintain order in society.

People need civil government just as much as they need food and drink every day. But over these necessities, civil government has a nobler task, namely, to uphold and glorify God's name. It must prevent people from blaspheming against God. In other words, civil government has the duty of rightly establishing true religion. Regarding civil government, Calvin divides the topic into three parts: the magistrate whose task is to keep and guard the laws, the laws with which the magistrate governs, and the people who are ruled by the law and who must obey the magistrate.

Looking at the role of the magistrate from a biblical point of view, Calvin attests that God confers the office's honor and dignity. The Bible shows that magistrates receive a mandate from God and that they represent God because they are given divine authority.

Calvin takes examples from the Old Testament in which judges were
appointed to rule cities or regions in Israel. In the New Testament
we read that Paul, too, is in support of civil government. In Romans 13
Paul writes clearly that the power of the government is an ordinance
from God and that it does not have any authority unless God gives
it. In other words, Paul teaches that civil government is ordained by
God. Consequently, civil magistrates must understand fully that
they must do the work of God, and therefore they must rule with
uprightness, prudence, gentleness, and self-control. They are the
vicars of God, and they should stand before the people with a full
understanding that they carry the duties that God himself gives to
them. With this in mind, Calvin encourages Christians to participate
actively in civil government. When Christians feel called to serve in
government, they must be encouraged to do so. He disagrees with
those, such as the Anabaptists, who think that Christians are forbidden to take part in civil government.

All civil governments must put in the foreground their main task,
namely, making piety their first concern. Therefore, when the government establishes rules and punishes wrongdoers, it must do so
as one who carries the judgment from God. To put this into a concrete application, Calvin shows that the law of God forbids people
from murdering others. In the case of murder, God gives civil government the power to punish murderers. Civil government is there
so that pious people do not have to enforce civil law. It is there by
the Lord's command to punish wrongdoers, which is not the role
of the church.

Calvin believes in what is often referred to as "just war." God
gives kings and other governmenxt leaders the authority to
maintain peace and order in their regions or dominions, to punish
evil deeds, and to restrain rioters.[13] They are also tasked to protect

[13]Calvin, *Institutes* IV.20.11.

their people from oppression by others. Because they function as defenders of the law, civil government also has the power to overthrow the efforts of evil people who want to corrupt the discipline of the laws. Following the same line of thought, Calvin says that when a foreign power tries to attack and invade another land, the government of the land has the authority to attack back in order to protect its own people. Kings or other leaders of a land are armed not just to restrain the misdeeds of their own people in the kingdom but also to defend their regions or countries when they are under an enemy's attack. To answer the objections of some Christians who disagree with the idea of a just war and cite passages in the Bible that forbid God's people from taking up arms, Calvin answers that these passages are intended to be used for the rule of the spiritual kingdom of Christ, not for the realm of human kingdoms on earth. He cites Luke 3:14, in which John the Baptist was asked by the soldiers what they must do. John said that they should not strike any person or do wrong to others, and they should feel content with their wages. John's reply here must have meant that these soldiers were allowed to carry out their duties as soldiers, which may have included going into war. The difference is that they do their duties on earth following the teaching of the kingdom of God. Civil magistrates must remember in carrying out their duties, including going to war, that they are not to be carried away with sinful desires, anger, and hatred. Following Augustine, Calvin reminds the people that civil government must still have pity on enemies. In addition, they must not initiate or look for reasons to enter into war. They may go into war only when they are hard pressed and driven into the situation, and they have no other solution to the conflict at hand.

Calvin is interested to show that Protestants can be good citizens, so he emphasizes that people must pay their taxes to the government. Taxes are lawful revenues for rulers, who can, in turn, do their work for the people. At the same time, however, leaders in government must also remember that money from taxes is not their personal money. Therefore, they must use it wisely and for the good of the people. They are responsible before God. Therefore, they must spend the money, which the people earn through their hard work, in service to God.

In the Old Testament, God gave Moses the law, and according to Calvin it could be categorized into moral, ceremonial, and judicial laws. We can summarize the moral laws as commands to worship God with a pure heart and to love others with sincere affection. The ceremonial laws were intended for the people of Israel; through these, God trained his people to follow him until the fullness of God would be manifested to all people and nations. The ceremonial laws that God gave to Israel foreshadowed the fullness that God would give to all people through Christ. The judicial laws in the Old Testament were for Israel's civil government. In these, God showed justice and equity so that Israel could live as a peaceful and just people. Ceremonial and judicial laws of the Old Testament are abrogated for us today, but their main principles remain. The ceremonial laws point to maintaining piety and worshiping God. The core of the judicial laws is love for one another.

Calvin sees the moral law in the Bible as giving testimony to the natural law. In the law of nature God has engraved a conscience in the minds of all people. For instance, the law of God in the Bible forbids stealing. But when we look at peoples and cultures around us, even when they do not know the Bible, they agree that stealing is morally wrong. The same also goes for the prohibitions against murder, against adultery, and against bearing false witness. Different nations may impose different kinds of punishments for those who trespass these laws, but they all know that these acts are wrong, because the natural law is set against them.

There are times when Christians need the help of the magistrate to settle matters pertaining to law and justice. Some Christians think that believers should not go to a civil court to settle a dispute. Calvin does not see harm in involving the judgment of the civil magistrate in such matters. Since God ordains the civil magistrate, he says that it can be helpful to settle lawsuits. In other words, Calvin reminds his readers that they may go to court, but not because of hatred and sinful desires against others. Lawsuits are permissible as long as they are used correctly—that is, following both the right use and the right order of the law. Those who think that they are wronged may sue, and those who are sued may present their defense. In this process, both parties must avoid fights and any desire to harm each other or to take revenge. He reminds people that no matter how just a lawsuit is, it will never be correctly prosecuted unless both parties treat each other with love and goodwill. Christians must always maintain peace and love toward each other, even in the case of a lawsuit.

Calvin's defense of the role of civil government becomes a greater challenge when people live under unjust rulers. History has shown us bad rulers who did not do their task according to God's laws, nor did they act as God's representatives for the people. Even in such bad cases, Calvin still maintains that these rulers are appointed by God and therefore still worthy of the respect of the people. He takes the example of King Nebuchadnezzar in the book of Daniel. There is no doubt that he was a bad ruler, but Daniel still obeyed the king. The task of the people is still to honor the ruler. God's authority and power will punish the bad ruler. In cases when people suffer because of evil rulers, the people can always come to God to ask for help, and God will help the people. The Bible has many instances in which God takes control and puts down such rulers. We all know the stories of Moses and Pharaoh, God's judgment on bad kings in the book of Judges, the deliverance that God brought to the people after they were exiled and enslaved in Babylon, and many others. In all these events, God, the greatest King, subdued lesser kings who did not obey his commands. In this explanation Calvin shows that the same principle still holds: people are called to be obedient to their government, and in turn the government must obey God. When the government fails to act according to God's design, God has the authority to punish the evil rulers. The people need only come to God for help.

Calvin concludes the *Institutes* with one important reminder: Christians' ultimate obedience is only to God, not to human rulers. They are not to exchange their total worship of God for devotion to their kings.[14] When Daniel was ordered not to pray to God but only to the king, he did not follow the order. He still prayed to God. As a consequence, Daniel was thrown into the lions' den. In all this, however, God was still in control over the king's power. Indeed, God delivered Daniel from the lions. Conversely, King Jeroboam ordered Israel to worship the golden calves, and the people followed the king's order. God was displeased with the people's obedience to the king. In the end, Calvin reminds his readers that we must obey God rather than human beings (Acts 5:29). This obedience may cause us suffering at the hands of evil rulers, but the truth remains: we have been redeemed by Christ at an enormous price. Therefore, we should not enslave ourselves under the desires of wicked people.

In Book Four of the *Institutes*, Calvin guides us to live out our faith. Having been redeemed by Christ, we walk with the Lord from day to day. God has provided us with the church, in which we can grow in faith, hear God's Word preached, and celebrate the sacraments. In the end, Calvin also leads us in thinking about what it means to live as Christians in the world. He explains that because

---

[14]Calvin, *Institutes* IV.20.32.

God ordains the government, we must obey it. While there are challenges we must face as Christians—including how we navigate our relationship with the government—ultimately our obedience is directed to God, who has created us and redeemed us.

Suggestions for Further Reading

Billings, J. Todd. *Calvin, Participation, and the Gift: The Activity of Believers in Union with Christ.* New York: Oxford University Press, 2007.

Burnett, Amy Nelson, ed. *John Calvin, Myth and Reality: Images and Impact of Geneva's Reformer.* Eugene, OR: Cascade, 2011.

Davis, Thomas J. *This Is My Body: The Presence of Christ in Reformation Thought.* Grand Rapids, MI: Baker Academic, 2008.

Horton, Michael. *Calvin on the Christian Life: Glorifying and Enjoying God Forever.* Wheaton, IL: Crossway, 2014.

Spierling, Karen. *Infant Baptism in Reformation Geneva: The Shaping of a Community, 1536–1564.* Louisville, KY: Westminster John Knox, 2009.

Conclusion

Throughout this book, I have tried to guide you to know John Calvin both as a man and as the author of his *magnum opus,* the final edition of *Institutes of the Christian Religion.* I hope by knowing him for who he was—in his struggles, challenges, and joys as he led the church in Geneva at the time of the Reformation—you have gained some insight into why and how he fought so persistently to reform the church and to ensure that the people of Geneva should live according to God's Word. I hope you find that he fulfilled God's call in his life, even as he faced turmoil such as family or personal issues, political or ecclesial matters, or physical illness. His life required him to make important and difficult decisions. And therefore his life was not unlike ours, even though today we live in different times and contexts.

By presenting Calvin in his historical, cultural, political, and theological contexts, I have meant to help you see him for who he was in his own time. Seeing him in this light checks our tendency to read our own situation and context into his writing, and thus incorrectly dictate our intentions into his writings or to interpret him based on what we want. Throughout his work, Calvin encountered many opponents. Sometimes, in defending his views—those he firmly believed were securely grounded on the Bible—he appeared too strong and relentless. But perhaps we can now see that he felt the need to defend his position against equally strong opponents. At the same time, the rhetoric of his day demanded that he did so. Disliking or dismissing his thoughts and beliefs based on his rhetorical style misses the target.

You have noticed, I'm sure, that Christians differ on some theological or doctrinal beliefs. In this book, I have mentioned some of them: issues concerning baptism, the Lord's Supper, the Trinity, predestination, and others. Calvin held his views on these doctrines dearly, and he was fully aware that others held their own positions. What I invite you to do, after reading this book, is to understand what he teaches and measure your own theological positions against his. You may find some similarities and some differences. This exercise will sharpen your own theological understanding as you get to know Calvin's. And by doing this, you will gain a deeper grasp of your own faith too. This was how I built my own theological views. While I find myself embracing much of what Calvin offers, there are places where I differ from him.

I hope that by now you have an overall picture of Calvin's theological system. While the details of his doctrines may be complicated, the overall picture is not too complex. When you look at this system closely, it stands on the knowledge of God and of ourselves, as Calvin clearly states in the opening of the *Institutes*. In that work, he leads us to understand that as we know God more deeply as Creator and Redeemer, we know ourselves better, too, as his creatures—created good, fallen, and therefore needing a Redeemer. And as we have a restored relationship with God in redemption through the sacrificial work of Christ, we live as God's children, worshiping him and joyfully celebrating the sacraments in the church.

Calvin's theological thoughts, particularly as he elaborates them in the *Institutes*, are still needed for us to live as Christians today. They provide a solid foundation for being a believer. I find his theological system to be consistent and coherent. Therefore, I also invite you to explore and understand his theology with all earnestness. I trust that doing so will help you to know and explain your own theological beliefs better.

While writing this book, I have reflected on my own theological journey and how I have traveled together with Calvin thus far. I am amazed to observe how much he has contributed to the church worldwide for more than four and a half centuries. All this time, Christians of all walks of life worldwide have embraced his teachings. The ecclesiastical practices and traditions that stemmed from his work in Geneva have inspired and influenced the way churches conduct their worship services. Books have been written on him and his theology, and I believe that many more will still be published far into the future. I thank God for giving us a thinker such as John Calvin. What a gift we have received because he was willing to listen to God's call.

General Index

Scripture Index

The Explorer's Guide Series

An Explorer's Guide to Karl Barth
978-0-8308-5137-9

An Explorer's Guide to Julian of Norwich
978-0-8308-5088-4